DELIVERING
on the
PROMISE

HOW TO ATTRACT, MANAGE,
AND RETAIN HUMAN CAPITAL

BRIAN FRIEDMAN
JAMES HATCH
DAVID M. WALKER

THE FREE PRESS

New York   London   Toronto   Singapore   Sydney

*f*P

THE FREE PRESS
A Division of Simon & Schuster Inc.
1230 Avenue of the Americas
New York, NY 10020

Manufactured in the United States of America

10 9 8 7 6 5 4 3 2 1

Library of Congress Cataloging-in-Publication Data
Friedman, Brian
    Delivering on the promise : how to attract, manage, and retain
human capital / Brian Friedman, James Hatch, David M. Walker.
        p.   cm.
    Includes bibliographical references and index.
    1. Personnel management.   2. Human capital.   3. Manpower planning.
I. Hatch, James.   II. Walker, David M.
III. Title.
HF5549.F7449   1998
658.3—dc21   98-36916
                                                          CIP

ISBN 1-4165-7357-7   ISBN 978-1-4165-7357-9

Contents

Preface

At Arthur Andersen, we "realize the value of people."™ This phrase is our motto, and the wellspring of our competitive advantage. As multidisciplinary and professional business advisors, we know both how to quantify the value of human resources and, more significantly, how to maximize that value, which we call *human capital*.

We recognize that people are assets that should be valued and developed, not resources that should be consumed. At the same time, people represent investments on which enterprises and shareholders should expect returns.

Delivering on the Promise contains no magic formulas, but it will help chief executives, senior human resources executives, and other managers get the most out of their companies' investments in human resources by enabling them to:

- align human capital programs with overall business strategy;
- evaluate the current worth of their human resources and the efficiency of their current human capital (HC) functions and programs;

- measure the amount of funds and time they are spending to source, develop, and manage these resources;
- assess the return on investment in human capital;
- manage and minimize the risks associated with the employment of people—the least predictable of all assets;
- maximize the value of human capital—the most valuable of all assets!

The first two chapters of this book will explore the past, present, and likely future of the human capital concept around the globe. Then, in its core offering, this guide will introduce the reader to a unique and proven process for human capital enhancement. To illustrate this process, we will offer examples based on our work with several leading companies. In our closing chapter, we will give brief descriptions of human capital initiatives at companies around the globe.

ORIGINS OF THIS BOOK

As consultants working for decades all over the world, we have seen problems—many of them easily avoidable—caused by a gap between strategic intention and practical action in companies. Mirroring this problem, the consulting arena itself has been split between high-level strategy development and highly technical implementation. This situation has created a vacuum for corporations and a race by consultants. This ground is now in turmoil as managers seek a useful way to align strategy and implementation in the vital human capital arena.

Arthur Andersen's proprietary, technically based approach is revealed here for the first time. Our previous publications (notably our *HR Director* series published in the United Kingdom and the United States) revealed only a few key aspects of our approach. Frankly, we were holding back—hesitant to reveal even a few of the "crown jewels" in our treasure chest of intellectual property. Now, however, our clients' pressing needs for a full, integrated approach has moved us to come forward with this "blue book."

By revealing more about our methods, we realize that we risk inviting our competitors and clients to practice these principles themselves, without our advice and guidance. More power to them! In our view, the need for proper values and direction in this area is so vast that there is more than enough opportunity for all of us to help where help is needed. As long as companies follow the principles espoused in this book, they will improve their ability to manage and retain human capital. By strengthening the overall health of the free enterprise system, our firm will benefit in the long run. Investors will get more than their fair share; they will get their just due. In addition, customers, workers, and other stakeholders will also benefit.

A WORD ON PROCESS

In describing our book, we have used the word "process" more than once, so it might be appropriate to define it. Rather than reinventing the wheel, we will quote the definition Michael Hammer uses in *Beyond Reengineering* (1996). He introduces the definition while pondering why so many corporate change initiatives fail.

> After a while, understanding gradually dawned on American managers: They were getting nowhere because they were applying task solutions to process problems.
>
> The difference between a task and process is the difference between part and whole. A task is a unit of work, a business activity normally performed by one person. A process, in contrast, is a *related group of tasks that together create a result of value to a customer*. . . . The problems that afflict modern organizations are not task problems. They are process problems. [Emphasis added.]

We at Arthur Andersen agree with this basic definition—but we would go one step further: Processes bring value not only to customers, but also to other stakeholders. As a firm, we can claim some very solid knowledge in this regard. Recently, based on decades of work in this area, we published a definitive list of organizational processes, listing 13 main processes (including several in the human resources arena) and 260 subprocesses. The Arthur Andersen Global Best Practices™ knowledge base, which we developed with the help of the International Benchmarking Clearinghouse in Houston, Texas, is a kind of Standard Industrial Classification Code of best practices around the world. This database, containing thirty thousand pages of case material in all aspects of business, and costing over $30 million to create, is the largest process-oriented database of management practices in the world.

One of the subprocesses we identified is the *process of change management itself.* The methodology described in this book summarizes what we have learned about this key process as it applies to all areas of human capital. By sharing our knowledge with you, we hope to guide you in creating more value, not only for customers but also for stockholders and, perhaps most important, employees themselves.

Acknowledgments

Shining Examples

"Thank me no thankings, nor proud me no prouds."

—William Shakespeare, *Romeo and Juliet*

As the named authors, we cannot receive full credit for this book, as many devoted and tireless people contributed to its creation. First, thanks are extended to Brett Walsh and Solange Charas, who made significant contributions to the structure and content of this book with their time, energy, expertise, and tireless reads and rereads of chapters.

Our gratitude must also be extended to Virginia Smith for her help with the logistics and management of the book-writing process, together with Bruce Meyer who also assisted in navigating the publishing world. Special thanks must also go to Jennifer Scheck and Marta Ward for their magnificent contributions.

Sincere appreciation to our colleague Charles Ketteman for his encouragement and guidance, and to all the members of his team for their help in designing and refining our methodologies and processes.

Last, unending thanks to our supremely competent wordsmith, Alexandra Lajoux, who was able to translate our theories and practice into a readable work.

Special thanks are extended to the families of the contributors of this book. We recognize that the time commitments required to make this book become a reality resulted in less time spent at home.

In their work for clients, and in their labors on this book, the people of Arthur Andersen exemplify the principles set forth in these pages. With the efforts and talents of the aforementioned individuals and their dedication to teamwork and results, we believe we have created a useful tool for managers to perform better in their jobs. We urge all managers to champion and apply the techniques described in this book.

Naturally, we hope to hear from you and *about* you, as your firm becomes a shining example, delivering on the promise of human capital, today and in the future.

Chapter One

HUMAN CAPITAL

From Promise to Reality

All organizations now say routinely, "People are our greatest asset." Yet few practice what they preach, let alone
truly believe it.

—Peter Drucker, "The New Society of Organizations,"
Harvard Business Review, September–October 1992

"People are our greatest asset." Do these words ring hollow for
you? If so, you are not alone. As Peter Drucker observed at the
dawn of this decade, this phrase has become a cliché—and borders on a
lie. Indeed, reengineering guru Michael Hammer has called it "the
biggest lie in contemporary American business," and it is hard to disagree. The seeming clash between company words and actions in the
human capital domain has embittered more than a few employees—and
has created ample material for mass media attacks on business. Turn on
any business show or flip to any business page, and no matter where you
are in the world, if the subject of employment comes up, you are likely
to hear charges of corporate hypocrisy.

How can companies truthfully say that they "value" employees, scold
the critics, if firms are willing to lay off thousands of workers to boost
share price? And how can employers claim that they put their employees "first," critics add, when the salary of a single CEO is higher than
the entire training budget for the next five years? Clearly, say these
doubters, human resources rank low in companies today—"just after
carbon paper," as the cartoon character Dilbert has observed.

But are companies really lying when they say that human resources are their greatest asset? Or are they merely indulging in some wishful thinking—asserting an ideal that *could* become a reality if given the proper tools? In our view, based on extensive work with major corporations and other organizations all over the world, the problem is not that companies *don't* value their people; it is that *they don't know how to*—they have not found a reliable way to appraise the worth of what they have, or to increase its value through better management.

This lack of know-how is not merely a problem for the "human resources department" (HR) to handle. Nor can it be blamed on HR. Human factors in the workplace cannot and should not be departmentalized—and thus marginalized. Because of its high impact on both company operations and on company value, this issue matters greatly to *all* managers and to boards of directors.

The message of this book is simple: In order to value people, companies must *move beyond the notion of human resources and toward the notion of human capital.* The very term *resource* (from the Latin *resurgere,* to rise again) implies an available supply that can be drawn upon when needed. In the corporate context, people seem like water in a well that will never run dry. Fire today, hire back tomorrow; easy come, easy go. But are people really a "resource" in this sense? Or are they more like a form of *capital*—something that gains or loses value depending on how much and how we invest in it?

In the following chapters, after a brief review of the history and current crisis state of human capital practices around the globe, we will introduce a unique and useful methodology for the management of human capital. This method, which we call Human Capital Appraisal™ (HCA™), shows how companies can increase the returns on their investments in the people they employ.

The model is based on five *stages* and five *areas* that can be visualized as a "5²" grid. As readers will see by turning to Chapter 3, the stages go from strategic clarification to assessment (including measurement of fit, cost, and value), to design, to implementation, and to monitoring against strategic goals. The areas span a full range from the actual movement of people in and out of organizations to the myriad systems that help them perform while they are there.

By having an overall sequence for measuring and enhancing human capital, and by including a full range of human capital areas in this process, companies can improve their returns on investment in this area—by far the most critical for companies today.

THE IDEA OF "HUMAN CAPITAL"

By its very name, the notion of "human capital" sees people not as a perishable resource to be consumed but as a valuable commodity to be developed. This idea is not entirely new. It dates back at least to the timeless Parable of the Talents told in the Judeo-Christian literature and no doubt in other cultures. (See Box 1-1.) For companies, the moral of the parable—and the moral of this book—is that *people become more valuable when we invest in them.* Moreover, *we can measure returns on*

BOX 1-1
The Parable of the Talents

A merchant had three servants and eight talents (silver coins) to distribute among them. He gave five talents to one servant and two talents to another servant. To the last servant he gave only one talent. The first two servants invested their money and doubled it, but the third servant buried his in the ground, where it gained no value. When the master returned, he praised the first two servants, and chastised the third. *

"So take the talent from him, and give it to the one with the ten talents. For to all those who have, more will be given, and they will have an abundance; but from those who have nothing, even what they have will be taken away. As for this worthless slave, throw him into the outer darkness, where there will be weeping and gnashing of teeth."

This parable has been interpreted traditionally to mean that people should exercise their personal abilities or "talents" in the world, rather than hoarding them. (Indeed, this story may have helped move the term "talent" into the realm of personal abilities.) But doesn't this parable have meaning in *companies* and other organizations as well? The first servant is like a company that has many high-caliber people and invests in all of them. The second servant is the same on a lesser scale. The third servant, alas, is like a company that has only a few good people and invests little in them.

*This opening paragraph is from Matthew 25: 28-30. The opening is paraphrased; the quote is verbatim. For more details, see the bibliography.

that investment. The significance of this insight should become more apparent after the following brief tour of the human capital notion.

A BRIEF HISTORY OF THE HUMAN CAPITAL CONCEPT

All human beings have intrinsic *value;* this idea is as old as written history. In the twenty-fourth century B.C., the Egyptian writer Ptahhotpe observed that even slave women—evidently the lowest rung of society in his day—might have something to contribute to society. ("Good speech is more hidden than malachite, yet it is found in the possession of women slaves at the millstones," he wrote.) In the thousands of years that have rolled by since this ancient Egyptian recorded his views, many great minds have expressed similar thoughts. It was not until the middle of the present millennium, however, that the notion of capital emerged—and, recently, the notion of human capital.

So what is human capital? Parsing the phrase can provide some answers.

Human (from the Latin *hominem,* for man) means of or relating to people. It signals our biological species: To be human is to be a person—not an animal, a god, a machine.

Capital (from the Latin *caput,* for head) has many nuances. In its simplest usage, it means the first, biggest, or best. In modern accounting, it means net worth—the remaining assets of a business after all liabilities have been deducted.

For the past three centuries, the notion of capital has evolved from the individual, to the corporation, to the national arena. (See Box 1-2.)

When first used in an economic context, the word capital meant wealth at the *individual* level. Randle Cotgrave's dictionary of the English and French languages, published in 1611, defines capital as "wealth, worth; a stocke; a man's principal or chief substance."

With the rise of joint stock companies in the seventeenth century, however, the term moved from the individual to the *organizational* realm. Capital, whether as an adjective modifying *stock* or as a noun in its own right, came to mean funds used to launch an enterprise (such as a joint stock company or a professional practice). Adam Smith, in *The Wealth of Nations* (1776), speaks of a company's "capital stock," and

---

BOX 1-2
Highlights in the History of "Capital"

1611 Randle Cotgrave defines "capital" as wealth owned by an individual.

1776–1790 Adam Smith and Edmund Burke write about "capital stock" of a company and the importance of beginning any enterprise ("trade") with "capital."

1793 Jeremy Bentham extends the notion of capital from the individual and company levels to the national level.

1867 Karl Marx asserts that all value comes from labor.

1911 Frederick Taylor's ideas compartmentalize labor, lessening its perceived value.

1979 Theodore Schultz and Sir Arthur Lewis receive the Nobel Prize in Economics for their pioneering work in human capital.

1998 In a *Chicago Tribune* obituary, Theodore Schultz is hailed as the "father of human capital." The notion of human capital has achieved wide recognition, with nearly two million Internet sites mentioning it.

Edmund Burke, in *The French Revolution* (1790), admonishes a man that he "began ill. . . . You set up your trade without a capital."

Soon the notion of capital transferred from the realm of the company to the even larger domain of the nation. The utilitarian economist Jeremy Bentham, in *Emancipation* (1793), speaks of capital as the money circulating in a nation. "In proportion to the quantity of capital a country has at its disposal, will . . . be the quantity of its trade."

By the early nineteenth century, the term extended beyond money or stock to value itself. Capital no longer meant merely funds, but something above and beyond funds—a unit of value linked to the work expended to create it. John Ramsay McCulloch, in *Principles of Political Economy* (1825), wrote of "the accumulation . . . of the *produce of previous labor,* or, as it is more commonly termed, of capital or stock." [Emphasis added.]

This linkage between money and work would take Europe by storm a few decades later in the most famous book ever written on the concept of capital—Karl Marx's *Das Kapital* (1867). In *Das Kapital* (or, in English, *Capital*), Marx argued that labor was the source of all value, and that investments made in land or technology only transferred value, but did not add value. He proposed communism as an economic system.

Marx declared this principle at the same time the Industrial Revolution was forcing an entirely different view in the capitalist world—the view that human beings were dispensable and interchangeable; that they were a necessary means to an end, not an end in themselves. It was in this dreary era that the notion of "human resources" was born. Jac Fitz-enz, founder of the Saratoga Institute in Saratoga, California, describes this genesis in his recent study, *How to Measure Human Resources Management:* "Since the value systems of nineteenth century industrialists focused on new ways to engineer and manufacture, the people function and the worker in general were not highly valued. Employees were treated like production parts and personnel like inventory clerks."

Ironically, it was the communist system that ultimately devalued human labor and ingenuity, and it was the capitalist system that increased its worth. Human capital has little meaning in a controlled economy; it can be the engine of wealth and growth in a free one. Yet during this waning twentieth century, capitalism has not achieved its full potential in this regard. We have had effective financial capitalism, but ineffective human capitalism. Even in highly developed modern economies such as the United States, the twentieth century has not completely broken away from the notion of the employee-as-commodity.

From Frederick Taylor's *Principles of Scientific Management* (1911) to Albert Dunlap's *Mean Business* (1998), the idea of human replaceability runs like a thin, darkening thread in the tapestry of industrial ideas—reminding individual employees ever more starkly of their relative unimportance in the grand scheme of corporate doings. At first the concept was more a theory than a practice. Through the 1960s, cradle-to-grave employment was the norm for many. By the 1970s, though, job security became job insecurity. We became, in the words of social scientist Warren Bennis of the University of Southern California, "the temporary society." Today, the concept of a "permanent job" has become an oxymoron. The closest we come to it is the "permatemp" notion—to use a term coined at Microsoft, the U.S. computer colossus.

No one has been spared this merciless notion—not even CEOs, whose average job tenure today is far shorter than in any past era. A bit of recent (late 1997) humor reveals CEO awareness of the trend. In accepting a well-deserved award from a group of peers (one of many that year), the CEO of a major public company had the room roaring with laughter when he ended his speech by reminding his listeners of the maxim, "Today a peacock, tomorrow a feather duster."

The Feather-Duster Phenomenon

The feather-duster phenomenon has persisted at all levels of corporate life despite other gains from the great managerial movements of the past few decades. Today's senior managers practiced *strategic planning* in the 1970s, *total quality management* (TQM) in the 1980s, and *reengineering* in the 1990s. Each of these movements made significant positive contributions to corporate performance, but as the old saying says, the good is often the enemy of the best. These movements—and countless others before them—could have had even *better* results if they had taken the value of human capital into full account.

In each of these movements, companies saw human resources as an interchangeable or even a disposable means to some greater end: market dominance, higher product and service quality, or more efficient processes. The great reality that all these movements missed was the fact that companies cannot achieve positive and lasting results unless they also learn to manage and enhance the value of their employees as a workforce.

Pursued apart from the basic issues of human capital, no corporate tool can work to its full effectiveness—not planning, not quality, not even reengineering, despite its measurable success. In fact, both Michael Hammer and James Champy have had to add a missing human element in recent sequels to *Reengineering the Corporation* (1993).

Their classic, now barely six years old, has sold over two million copies worldwide, and companies that followed its advice have done measurably better. By overhauling and restructuring companies to respond to change in service of customers, adherents of reengineering have improved their efficiency and their financial performance. Nonetheless, both authors have issued corrective postscripts.

In *Reengineering Management: The Mandate for New Leadership* (1995), Champy declared in his very first sentence: "Reengineering is in trouble." Although the ideas of reengineering are sound, Champy said, managers resist applying them. Therefore, he said, management itself—not just companies—must be reengineered. In *Beyond Reengineering: How the Process-Centered Organization is Changing Our Work and Our Lives* (1996), Hammer added another twist. The original reengineering book and movement had been about reengineering tasks; the new reengineering, he said, will be about reengineering processes.

These postreengineering guides contain much wisdom, but they continue to assume an unlimited supply of qualified personnel as a backdrop to management creativity. Thus, still today, to finish the Drucker quote we began earlier, "Managers still believe, though perhaps not consciously, what nineteenth-century employers believed: people need us more than we need them."

Do you as a manager or director believe this? If so, you are missing a key part of the concept of human capital: *companies need people*. To say that there is human capital within a company (or other organization) implies many things:

- Human beings employed in their work are not merely people moving assets around—they themselves are assets that can be *valued, measured,* and *developed like any other asset held by the corporation.*
- Human beings are dynamic assets that can increase in value over time, not inert assets that depreciate in value.
- Human beings are *prime among all assets.* Capital, remember, is synonymous with net worth—the remaining assets of a business after all liabilities have been deducted.
- As such, human beings and the systems created to recruit, reward, and develop them form a *major part of any company's value*—as much or more than other assets such as cash, land, plants and equipment, and intellectual property.
- Company value, and therefore *shareholder value* (the value of a company's stock), can suffer when human capital is mismanaged.

Over the past few decades, ideas like these have been slowly gaining acceptance in the marketplace. In corporations around the globe, running alongside the dark thread of human replaceability has been the bright thread of human value—and its growth over time in the form of human capital. Although there is no single accepted definition of human capital, there is a growing recognition that the old notion of human resources and the old way of managing those resources no longer serve the purpose of the modern company.

CHALLENGES TO HUMAN CAPITAL

In private conversation at a recent gathering of U.S. corporate directors, a manufacturing executive made this observation:

> Companies are willing to invest millions in machines, which depreciate in value over time, but they are reluctant to make an equivalent investment in people, who appreciate in value over time. For me, there is no contest. I would rather spend $10,000 in training now and have it be worth $100,000 or more in 10 years, than invest $100,000 in a machine that will be worth $10,000 or less in 10 years.

This executive did not need a book to tell him this—he knew it from his experience. His idea is so simple, so sensible, so true. Why then do companies still see employees as resources to be mined rather than as capital to be developed?

We see two main sets of challenges impeding the spread of the human capital notion: first, limitations imposed by measurement and accounting systems; and second, limitations imposed by managers themselves—both in their perspective and in their motivation.

Challenge One: Limitations of Measurement and Accounting Systems

The notion of capital is an accounting notion, yet there is no standard way of measuring its value—and no current movement to do so. As such, the notion of human capital has remained a vague concept rather than a sharp tool. One might exuberantly call for the accounting profession to recognize human capital—as consultant Kevin Thomson (1998) recently did in calling for recognition of *emotional capital*—but this may not be realistic, at least in the near term.

As partners in one of the world's oldest and largest accounting and consulting firms, we appreciate the broadly collective and deeply traditional nature of accounting. To become "generally accepted" in a nation—much less around the globe—new principles must go through many years of dialogue and refinement. Consider, for example, the notion that derivative financial instruments should be valued at their market value. In the United States, it took the Financial Accounting Standards Board (FASB) ten years before it passed a rule based on this concept.

If it takes a decade to pass a new rule on a point that concerns only a minority of companies, how much more time would a change in mandatory accounting for human capital take? We do not expect to see it in our working lifetimes. Nonetheless, companies can begin measuring and reporting on human capital on a voluntary basis in their financial statements. Throughout this book, we will offer tools and concepts that will be useful in pursuing this goal.

Challenge Two: Limitations of Managerial Perspective and Motive

The tougher challenge is the challenge of perspective. Managers often find it difficult to assess human capital within their own organizations because they are a vital part of that capital—connected to that capital through the work of the organization and through direct reporting lines. This makes it very difficult to take an objective stance in relation to a company's human capital as a whole, or from programs created to obtain, manage, and enhance it. How can one be at arm's length from an entity that includes oneself?

Beyond the challenge of managerial perspective is the related challenge of managerial motive. Change is difficult for everyone, including the managers in charge of it. Why should managers change their view of employees—seeing them as valuable capital rather than as expendable resources—when the old view of HR is serving them well enough today? Why should companies shake up their functionary HR operations as long as they are doing an adequate job? The bad news is that some HR managers will never change unless they have to. The good news is that the time has come: Managers must rise to the human capital concept or sink in the wake of its arrival.

HUMAN CAPITAL ARRIVES

Yes, the notion of human capital has arrived—en masse. The Amazon site on the World Wide Web lists over two hundred books addressing the subject. Although many of these use the old human resources terminology, there is growing evidence even in these that the term is taking hold. The Lexis-Nexis database (also on the Web) lists over four hundred articles on the topic. And for every word in print, there are hundreds in the technosphere. According to the popular Netfind search engine, the phrase "human capital" appears now in nearly *two million* websites around the world.

With this great abundance of materials, can there be anything new to say? The answer is yes. A recent posting on the Internet (from www.csu.edu, found in January 1998) says it all:

> Are there any studies (beside macroeconomic) which show that investing in human capital directly produced a financial return on investment? I am trying to encourage an employer to make an investment in his people, both in terms of job-related training, and personal development.

Clearly, despite all the information available, individuals like the anonymous one making this posting still need to prove to their employers or (if they are advisers) clients that human beings merit investment. *Human capital today is a concept in search of a context.*

Fortunately, this context is emerging. Researchers are beginning to provide quantitative proof that investments in human resources pay off.

For many years, efforts to measure returns on investment in human capital seemed doomed to failure. Early attempts to correlate human capital investments with stockholder returns came to naught. For example, in their 1977 paper, "Human Capital and Capital Market Equilibrium," Eugene F. Fama of the University of Chicago and William Schwert of the William E. Simon School of the University of Rochester found that:

extending popular two-parameter models of capital market equilibrium to allow for the existence of non-marketable human capital does not provide better empirical descriptions of the expected return-risk relationship for marketable securities than those that come out of simpler models.

Why? Because:

relationships between the return on human capital and the returns on various marketable assets are weak, so that the model that includes human capital leads to estimates of risk for marketable assets indistinguishable from those of simpler models.

This paper threw down a gauntlet that said, in effect, "We dare you to find a correlation between company value and investments in people." Many scholars have taken up this challenge in succeeding years; the Fama-Schwert paper has been cited in at least thirty-six scholarly papers since then, by Schwert's count (recorded on his website at Rochester).

Meanwhile, on the macroeconomic front, the importance of human capital was beginning to surface in a big way. In 1979, the Nobel Prize in Economics was awarded to Theodore Schultz of the University of Chicago and Sir Arthur Lewis of Princeton University for their revolutionary theories of labor cost. Their writings disputed the old idea of a fixed supply of labor. Labor may be scarce or abundant—and in some economies unlimited—they said, affecting labor costs. The disparity between developed nations with their limited supplies of labor and less developed nations with their unlimited supply has created a kind of modern-day economic colonialism. Schultz and Lewis both wrote many papers exploring the implications of this dynamic.

Although neither of these insightful economists is alive today—Lewis died in 1990 and Schultz died in 1998—their legacy lives on. The February 28, 1998, *Chicago Tribune* obituary for Schultz hails him as "the father of human capital." The description is no exaggeration—although the concept of human capital has been slow to catch on. From 1979 to 1989, relatively few articles and books gave serious attention to human capital (among them Schultz's *Investing in People,* published in 1982). But in the 1990s, the idea of human capital began to catch on. In

1992, Gary Stanley Becker won the Nobel Prize in Economics for his own theories of human capital, helping to fuel continued interest in the concept. A geometric growth pattern of articles on the topic began that continues to this day, with every year matching or doubling previous records. (See Box 1-3.) If current trends continue, there could be well over one hundred articles on human capital appearing in periodicals during 1998 alone.

Most of these articles address only macroeconomic issues of national policy education or labor, often in a narrow context—studying, for example, "dental hygienists" or "low-income workers in Bombay." Only a few have taken a microeconomic view that could help an individual company and its managers. For these articles, as well as macroeconomic treatments of the subject, see the Bibliography. The main gist of these microeconomic articles is that it is better to invest in human capital than to reduce or replace it.

A RESEARCH REVIEW

Over the past few years, several scholars have had success in finding correlations between investments in human capital and company performances. (See Box 1-4.)

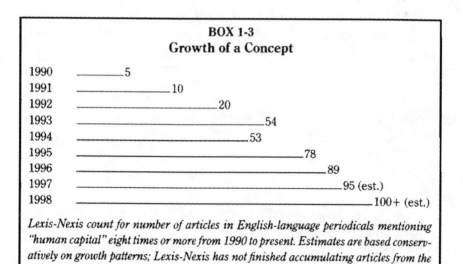

BOX 1-3
Growth of a Concept

1990	5
1991	10
1992	20
1993	54
1994	53
1995	78
1996	89
1997	95 (est.)
1998	100+ (est.)

Lexis-Nexis count for number of articles in English-language periodicals mentioning "human capital" eight times or more from 1990 to present. Estimates are based conservatively on growth patterns; Lexis-Nexis has not finished accumulating articles from the years estimated.

BOX 1-4
Landmark Human Capital Research

Cascio (1995) showed the negative effects of massive downsizing.

Huselid (1995) found lower staff turnover, higher sales per employee, and higher stock price/book value ratios for firms that had programs to develop and motivate employees.

Bilmes (1996) found a high correlation between improvement in returns to shareholders and investment in both traditional and "intrapreneurship" programs.

Welbourne and Andrews (1996) showed longer post-IPO survival rates for companies that invest in human capital.

Families and Work Institute (1998) linked job satisfaction and firm profits to workplace support, including flexibility, family-friendly policies, and other factors.

Cascio

In a Brookings Institution colloquium on the state of human capital in the mid-1990s, Jonathan Low, deputy assistant secretary for work and technology policy at the U.S. Department of Labor, reported that five different groups were planning to set up screens or create funds based on workplace practices and investments in human capital. Low cited a study by Wayne Cascio of the University of Colorado on the negative effects of massive downsizing. Three years after downsizing, sample companies had subsequent earnings increases of 183 percent, whereas comparable firms in the same industries that did not downsize had earnings increases of 422 percent. Cumulative stock returns over three years were 4.7 percent vs. 34.3 percent. Low concluded that pension fund managers "would be justified in encouraging a second look at such tactics."

Huselid

Other studies, recently highlighted by Stanford University professor Jeffrey Pfeffer in *The Human Equation: Building Profits by Putting People First* (1998), show similar results. Pfeffer cites Mark Huselid (1995), whose study of 3,452 firms found lower staff turnover, higher sales per employee, and higher stock price/book value ratios for firms that had programs to develop and motivate employees, and programs to link employee performance to pay and promotions.

Firms with practices designed to increase employees' on-the-job knowledge, skills, and abilities and to reward on-the-job achievements clearly outperform their peers without such practices. Statistically speaking, a single standard deviation increase in such practices led to a 7.05 percent decrease in employee turnover, $27,044 more in sales per employee, $3,814 more in profits per employee, and $18,641 more in market value or "shareholder wealth" per employee. A more recent study by Huselid (1997), conducted in the bull market of the 1990s, found even more dramatic results for stock values—a $41,000 increase per employee.

Bilmes

Ongoing research by Linda Bilmes, a former consultant with a Big Six accounting firm and now a U.S. deputy secretary of commerce, shows that companies with "employee-friendly" policies do better than peer companies lacking such policies. In a pilot study with consultants based in Germany (Bilmes et al. 1996), she studied one hundred German companies from 1987 to 1994, measuring employee focus in terms of both traditional human resources policies and opportunities for "intrapreneurship" within the company.

Traditional HR policy measures were as follows:

- The extent to which the corporate philosophy recognizes the contribution of employees as reflected in mission statements and publications.
- The number of layoffs relative to the industry average and efforts to help relocate redundant employees.
- General human resources policies, including recruitment, performance evaluation and feedback, and promotion opportunities.
- The expenditures per employee on training, and continuing levels of training.

Intrapreneurship measures were as follows:

- The flexibility of work hours.
- Project organization, including the prevalence of teams, number of levels of hierarchy (the fewer the better), and independence of working units.
- The opportunities for employees to learn skills in new areas and the speed with which a firm can transfer staff to new fields.
- The extent to which employees share in company performance through profit sharing, performance pay, and bonuses.

Bilmes and her colleagues found a high correlation between improvement in returns to shareholders and investment in both traditional and intrapreneurship programs. Unfortunately, the Bilmes study also found that relatively few companies are making this investment at a significant level. Right now, Bilmes is broadening her research to cover a wider span of countries.

Welbourne and Andrews

In a study of five-year survival rates for companies going public in 1988, Theresa Welbourne and Alice Andrews (1996), also cited in Pfeffer, found higher survival rates for companies that have (based on their prospectuses and other public disclosures):

- Strategy and mission statements citing employees as a competitive advantage.
- Employee training programs.
- A company official responsible for human resources management.
- A relatively high level of full-time rather than temporary or contract workers.
- High self-assessment on employee relations.

They also found higher survival rates for companies that have broader participation in such initiatives as stock ownership, gain sharing, and stock option awards.

In addition to citing these general studies, Pfeffer cites more focused research on the apparel, automobile, oil refining, semiconductor, service, and steel-manufacturing industries to show dramatic results. His conclusion: "Substantial gains, on the order of 40 percent or so in most of the studies reviewed, can be obtained by implementing high performance management practices."

Families and Work Institute

In April 1998, the *Families and Work Institute* released a study linking job satisfaction to workplace support. When asked what contributed to their sense of well-being on the job, 37 percent of employees cited work conditions, such as flexibility, family-friendly policies, supervisor support, and lack of discrimination. The study, entitled *National Study of the Changing Workforce*, also linked worker-friendly programs to profitability.

THE CURRENT "CRISIS" STATE OF HUMAN CAPITAL

Clearly, the high value of human capital—and the heavy cost of neglecting it—is not a matter of emotion or faith, though both of these realms will always give clues in support of human value. Rather, the value of human capital is a matter of hard-and-fast economics.

As we approach the twenty-first century, as outlined in Chapter 2, relatively stable economies such as Europe and North America are experiencing low rates of unemployment, inflation, and interest—creating a rare golden age in some countries. Meanwhile, even in the currently unstable economies of parts of Asia, heavy foreign investment continues, indicating confidence and facilitating recovery. Given the growing importance and scarcity of human capital and the plenitude of financial capital, companies worldwide will have a natural tendency to use financial capital to obtain and leverage their human capital.

This new appreciation of human capital could reverse the dangerous course that business has taken over the past few decades. In his new book, *The Loyalty Effect,* Frederick F. Reichheld documents a lack of loyalty throughout the corporate world, with a growing mistrust between corporations and employees. But rather than condoning this trend as most business observers do today, he decries it:

> Some executives are concluding that the corporations of the future—in the postcapitalist society—will need to be more like nomadic tribes, pitching

their tents anywhere on a moment's notice, and less like plodding agriculturists, rooted to one place and one core competence. This may seem a reasonable response to the increasing disorder and confusions of the business world. And the picture it paints of dynamic flexibility and adventurous energy may be very attractive. But consider how little progress nomadic tribes have made compared to the great civilizations with their enduring institutions, their sciences and cities, their ability to cope with change from a stable base.

Reichheld has put his finger on the pulse of a problem, but it may be worse than he thinks. Comparing the fast-changing companies to nomadic tribes may be too kind. Tribes—nomadic or not—have a measure of stability and unity in their leadership, their populations, and their values. Many companies today show no such stability—least of all in their treatment of human capital. The current state of human capital is in crisis in the true sense of the word, tracing to its Greek roots—*krinein*, to separate. A crisis is a time when elements that were formerly unified have fallen apart and need to be rejoined. How true this is of human capital today!

In a growing number of accounting, consulting, investment banking, and law firms, ruthless raids on talent have become an accepted business practice as victims turn into perpetrators just to survive. (As one raid-plagued consultant recently vowed, "I'm going to do to them what they've done to me.") What can break this vicious cycle?

It bears repeating: the value of companies can suffer when human capital is mismanaged—that is, when the *stages* of the human capital management process are not aligned with the *areas* within that process. In the following chapters, after a brief review of worldwide human capital trends, we offer both positive and negative examples of this truth as we present our Human Capital Appraisal™ approach—a new way to restore wholeness to human capital.

CONCLUSION

In order to value people, companies must move beyond the notion of human resources and toward the notion of human capital, a notion that sees people not as a perishable resource to be consumed but as a valuable commodity to be developed. This concept has been developing gradually for centuries, ever since collective enterprises began. In recent decades, despite continuing allegiance to older ideas, we have seen a gradual rise in commentary and research on this topic—including most recently the finding that investments in human capital result in higher returns to shareholders.

Such findings place companies at a crossroads. Clearly, investments in human capital pay off. The question is, how should these investments be made, and how can return on these investments be measured? The question has become increasingly urgent at this time, when economic fundamentals and current "hot" business issues point to a scarcity of human capital in the developed world. The remainder of this book offers information and resources that can help managers realize the full value of human capital in their organizations.

Chapter Two

GLOBAL HUMAN CAPITAL

A World of Wealth

No man is an island, entire of itself; every man is a piece
of the continent, a part of the main.

—John Donne, *Devotions Upon Emergent Occasions*

In March 1998, the government of China made a stunning announcement. In response to slow economic growth, said the Beijing authorities, China would reduce the number of government employees by up to *four million*—half of its eight million head count. The move was part of an overall plan, as the Associated Press reported, to "reduce waste and improve efficiency in government and industry" in response to slow economic growth.

For many observers, the event symbolized the futility of economic planning in the human resources arena. Just as printing more money cannot create more financial capital, designating more jobs can never create more human capital. To create and sustain lasting structures for human initiative, whether in the public sector or the private sector, managers must be *free to manage*—to create and sell products and services with a workforce that is built person by person and strategy by strategy.

The downsizing of the state bureaucracy in China also revealed another imperative—the need to *manage globally*. Chinese companies may have global customers, but they employ only domestic workers—limiting their global reach. Today, thanks to new technology and the increasing liberalization of trade, even relatively small companies around the world are learning that they can become truly worldwide in their reach—not merely exporting, importing, or franchising, but creating worldwide, integrated human capital systems.

HUMAN CAPITAL: A WORKING DEFINITION

And so a new challenge is riveting the attention and driving the efforts of business managers around the world—the goal of employing, retaining, and motivating the best of the best at every level without regard for geographic boundaries to fulfill changing strategic objectives. Managers everywhere are coming to understand the great difference between human resources—merely drawing from an available labor pool—and human capital—the transformation of people into market power through strategy-driven programs. At Arthur Andersen, this is not the future—it is the present, for ourselves (see Box 2-1) and for our clients.

Gone are the days when our clients operated in a single country, and asked for help there. Today, most of our clients have global reach and expect our firm to have it, too. A typical client request: "We have employees in fifty countries—and we need a stock-based incentive program that works the same for all of them. Assign us your top share-plan experts. We don't care where they are located—as long as they can do the job globally."

BOX 2-1
Arthur Andersen: A Global Operation

Arthur Andersen operates around the globe—with 363 offices in 78 countries. More important, we also *build human capital* worldwide. Serving over 80,000 clients and generating over $5.2 billion in annual revenues, we are one of the world's largest providers of professional services. Arthur Andersen devotes over 6 percent of its gross earnings to training (high by any industry standard)—virtually all of it to build international teams.

As part of Arthur Andersen, the Human Capital Services practice also operates worldwide. In Asia, Australia, Europe, North America, and South America, we have a variety of professionals, from compensation consultants to strategy, tax, actuarial, and investment specialists—all working on global issues for human capital.

Clients that lack global capabilities are eager to build them. Very recently one of our clients—a leader in a service business—came to us with an urgent dilemma. Its own top client was about to drop its account with this service provider because it was not global enough. Our client had been providing multinational services through a patchwork of national franchises built up through acquisition. But it was not really delivering an integrated global service. Its number-one customer complained, "We want service all over the world—and we want one account manager for it, not a dozen." We are working with our client to turn its far-flung employee base into one integrated team.

This challenge confronts companies all around the world, despite differing conditions. In Asia, government downsizing in China and a financial crisis in Southeast Asia have triggered unprecedented waves of job relocation and loss, surely the most fundamental of all human capital concerns. A continent away, companies are facing an array of emerging financial and legal issues as they manage human capital in the European Union, still a new playing field after less than a decade of juridical life. Meanwhile, in North America, managers are beginning to evaluate and value their human capital as never before, as sustained prosperity shifts the corporate focus from downsizing to retention and recruitment.

In each of these regions, the burning questions are different; issues that buffet managers in one economic hemisphere may barely ruffle their peers in another—and vice versa. But although their concerns differ, their fates are one. Our increasingly global economy ensures that no nation and no company suffers or triumphs alone. Moreover, in this new global economy, certain *core principles* are emerging to guide managers as they turn local human resources into global human capital.

Prosperity Principle One: Freedom to Manage

One core principle is the growing conviction that *managers must be free to manage*—that is, economic prosperity depends on the freedom of the private economic sector. This is an opening message of the *1998 Index of Economic Freedom,* an economic bellwether copublished for the last four years by the Heritage Foundation, a think tank in Washington, D.C., and the *Wall Street Journal.* The back-cover copy of this book rightly notes the importance of economic liberty:

> From the Asian tigers to the ex-socialist states of Central Europe to the most desperate outposts of Africa, the economic catchword of our era is freedom. Around the globe, policymakers and investors increasingly understand that economic growth depends on economic freedom. To be free is to grow and prosper.

The *Index* has scored 156 countries based on several indicators, including lack of centralized controls on business management practices. Index categories do not correlate strictly to more traditional notions of degrees of development or the "first," "second," and "third" economic worlds. Instead, they are based on degrees of market freedom.

Index economists have shown a strong correlation between economic freedom and economic prosperity—measured both in terms of gross domestic product (GDP) per person, and in terms of the growth in individual income. For example, long-run average annual per capital GDP growth is 2.88 percent for "free" countries, 0.97 percent for "mostly free" countries, −0.32 percent to "mostly unfree" countries, and −1.44 percent for "unfree countries." A score of "free" or "mostly free" indicates good long-term prospects for national prosperity and, as part of that, company value.

Prosperity Principle Two: Global Management of Human Capital

A related core principle that is dawning on managers around the world is the fact that *the health of free enterprise depends in large part on people—* the day-to-day, decade-to-decade management of human talent and effort around the world. If managers are free to manage their human capital in response to changing global markets, and if they follow such freedom with global action, then economic growth and prosperity will follow.

Not surprisingly, *Index* editors list "investing in human capital" and "allowing free trade" as two of the six fundamental actions (along with accumulating financial capital, keeping government small, respecting property and law, and refraining from excessive regulation) that can lead to economic growth around the world. By investing in human capital, they mean training to increase worker productivity. By allowing free trade they mean opening the country to foreign trade and investment—including the ability to build new companies or purchase existing ones. Free trade brings several benefits, say the new growth economists—including faster and deeper diffusion of technology from abroad. This is a key point for all companies today, given the tremendous imbalance in technological savvy—for example, the all-important Internet—from region to region.

The *Index* is based on sound theory—a "new growth theory" of economics that says economic systems (which can be regions, countries, industries, or companies) need not be locked into recurring boom and bust cycles. Rather, economies *can* continue to grow profitably for an *indefinite period.* The old idea of economic cycles was based on a presumption of decreasing (or diminishing) returns. What went up had to come down. The new economics argues that it is possible to sustain prosperity by following certain principles—including *investment in human capital*—but only in a voluntary, market-driven mode, never by force.

THE FREEDOM TO MANAGE: A POWERFUL PARADOX

The simple fact is that *free markets reward company investments in human capital.* In Chapter 1 we presented strong empirical evidence for this proposition, citing numerous studies showing that organizational and national prosperity depend on the value of human capital. But how can this value be realized? History proves that it cannot be achieved by force—not by central governments, and not by company headquarters. This is the grand paradox the world economy faces at the dawn of this new millennium. Attempts to force companies to value their human capital are doomed to failure; the incentive must come from within—from the needs imposed by a company or divisional strategy that takes account of market forces.

This is not to say that government has no role whatsoever in influencing employment conditions in a free economy. Our definitions of freedom (and the *Index*'s scores) are formed in a world where employers all work against a minimum baseline of mandated standards. As Pfeffer (1998) has noted, governments in virtually all countries have laws or policies for minimum wages, maximum work hours (overtime), collective bargaining, occupational safety, occupational health, and child labor, among other universal standards of work-life decency.

Moreover, certain government initiatives that encourage *voluntary* initiatives by employers can create the climate and communications links necessary for concerted action on a particular front. Notable examples include the former Office of the American Workplace in the United States and the ongoing Investors in People program in the United Kingdom. These programs do not mandate standards but rather recognize companies that conformed to certain benchmarks. Both programs have successfully promoted higher awareness of the impact that good employee management can have on company performance. Moreover, there is documented evidence that participants in both programs improved their financial performance.

The key here, again, lies in the word *voluntary.* We repeat: Managers must be free to manage. Our experience all over the world shows that the systems used for developing human capital can make a critical difference in the survival and success of companies. Technology and markets are changing so fast that companies need to be in a state of change readiness, and they need the freedom and flexibility to change in every area, from recruitment to compliance. They must invest in their human capital—but the nature of their investment must be driven by market conditions and company strategy, not government policy.

In this opinion, we seem to be staking out a position as contrarians against a different prevailing view. In preparing this book, we drew mainly from the most primary resource of all—our firm's direct experience with thousands of executives in hundreds of firms over decades of experience in both the private and public sector. We also read or revisited scores of books and articles in the field of human resources.

In these secondary resources, we found a significant pattern. Almost invariably, authors cite evidence that good employment practices (defined in various ways) are linked to good financial performance (also defined in various ways). They usually go on to note that despite this evidence, most companies do not follow the benchmark practices studied. And they often conclude that certain practices should be mandated or strongly encouraged by government.

In our experience—and we believe we speak for our clients as well, here—this conclusion misses the real point. Although voluntary government programs can do considerable good, they will never be the key to financial success. What drives business executives (as opposed to academics or consultants) is, was, and ever shall be *strategy*, not standards. That is, if you tell managers to do something because it is the decent thing to do and others have made money doing it, they may take the action, but they are unlikely to "run with it"—to go beyond it to create new levels of performance.

We have seen time and time again that businesses tend to rise to government-set maximums and sink to government-set minimums—exactly the opposite of the behavior wished. For example, the million-dollar CEO paycheck was not widespread in the United States before the government added Section 162 (m) to the Internal Revenue Code restricting the tax deductibility of pay over the million-dollar mark. Suddenly, it seemed that every CEO in America expected to be at or close to that ceiling!

Worse yet, businesses begin to design their programs around government mandates, rather than basing their programs on market trends and business needs. For example, demographic projections reveal that labor shortages and skills gaps are likely to become much more acute and widespread beginning around 2011. While many government-sponsored retirement programs give individuals the ability to retire at relatively young ages (62 for early retirement under the U.S. Social Security System), companies may need to encourage their workers to stay in the workforce longer in the years ahead. Businesses must determine their own retirement and other human capital strategies, rather than letting government do this for them.

By contrast, if business leaders give managers an overall goal to achieve, and provide them with human resources, policy tools, and incentives to achieve it, no one will be able to stop them as they "go for it" in dynamic, creative, and market-driven ways.

In the following chapters, we will propose a *strategy-driven process* that can help managers improve the link between strategic goals and human resources—and thus create valuable human capital.

Before we describe this process, though, let us look at the wealth it can create. In the following brief world tour, we will see a correlation between economic freedom, including voluntary, market-driven investment in human capital, and prosperity. We will travel from Asia, now engaged in massive labor downsizing, to Europe, where employment rates are steady, to the United States, currently riding a wave of labor growth. And everywhere we go, we will see how critical the market-based management of human capital can be in determining the wealth of nations (to use Adam Smith's enduring phrase) and the wealth of companies.

THE ASIAN OUTLOOK

Even as we attempt to comment on the "Asian Outlook," we must admit that there is no such thing. Asia can no longer be viewed as a single region or accumulation of countries with similar opportunities and problems.

In the past few decades, the free-market countries of Asia have grown from virtually undeveloped economies to economic superpowers, each with a unique claim to greatness. As historians have chronicled copiously, they did this through a combination of hard work, thrift, and market perspicacity. Then, in the summer of 1997, just before the Year of the Tiger began, Asia's fortunes began to turn. Many weak banks failed, markets lost confidence, and negative results began to snowball: falling currency rates, falling stock prices, more business failures, growing unemployment . . . the woes seemed to be marching in relentless lockstep, and they continue as we go to press. As of June 1, 1998, Japan's unemployment rate was 4.1 percent—the highest level in over 20 years. Not surprisingly, Japanese consumers have stayed away from major purchases. May 1998 marked the fourteenth consecutive month of falling automobile and truck sales. Financial indicators were no better in mid-1998. The Nikkei Stock Average and the Tokyo Stock Price Index were both losing points, the yen was falling against the dollar, and the yield on the benchmark 10-year Japanese government bond was at a record low.

Asian economies affected by the current financial crisis include the southeastern nations of Indonesia, Malaysia, Singapore, the Philippines, Taiwan, and Thailand, as well as their neighbor to the north, South Korea. Also affected is nearby Hong Kong, a Special Administrative Area within China that remains a financial hub following decades of economic freedom under British rule until July 1997. In Japan, a banking crisis seems to be looming, and the Tokyo stock market shows signs of weakness, with dramatic price drops in 1998—one so bad they called it the "Big Bang."

Yet most experts believe that Asia's downturn is temporary. They point to continuing investments in Asian companies, a sign of confidence in the economy. With all the internal indicators pointing south, what accounts for this optimism on the part of foreign investors? One reason is confidence in the long-term *value of human capital* these regions possess, thanks to their free-market economies.

The *Index* lists Hong Kong and Singapore as the two most free economies in the world. This result might seem surprising, since the "mostly unfree" China now has authority over Hong Kong, but economically speaking, China has let Hong Kong operate as it did before the transition to Chinese rule, the *Index* notes. Together with Taiwan, Hong Kong and Singapore constitute three of only nine economies considered truly "free" by *Index* standards. (The others are Bahrain, Luxembourg, New Zealand, Switzerland, the United Kingdom, and the United States.) In these countries, managers have the flexibility to manage financial and human capital as they see fit in response to market conditions, with relatively low controls set by external planners.

Other Asian economies ranking relatively high in the *Index* scores included (in descending order of freedom) Japan, South Korea, Malaysia, Thailand, the Philippines, and Indonesia—all in the "free" or "mostly free" range. In many of these countries, employees could expect employment for life—not because of government mandates but rather because of managerial values. As economic forces disrupt this practice, Asian business will be put to the test: Will they keep their faith in free markets for human capital?

China, as mentioned, appears in the "mostly unfree" range. Yet the recent move by the Chinese government to scale down its own size may be a harbinger for greater freedom in the future—and thus greater prosperity. If companies in Asian countries use their freedom to become truly global companies—rather than mere exporters or multinationals—they will not only survive but thrive in a changing world economy.

THE EUROPEAN OUTLOOK

In Europe as elsewhere, as John Donne wrote, "no man is an island." Continuing that sentiment, we would affirm with Donne that "if a clod be washed away by the seas, Europe is the less." For just as Europe needs all its earth, it needs all its human capital. Indeed, at its origin, the word *human* means "of the earth," deriving from the Latin word *humus.* So what is the current outlook for human capital in Europe? To find out, let us begin by taking a look at the collective business conditions for the fifteen member nations of the European Union (EU).

Managers in Europe must cope with two sources of baseline standards for employee management—their own national laws, and the laws of Europe. The European Commission (EC) in Brussels, which sets standards for EU members, has issued a number of initiatives affecting labor practices. Although many of these encourage member countries to adopt directives early on a voluntary basis, many directives eventually become mandatory. For example, the European Works Council Directive began as a voluntary measure in 1994, is now in a negotiable period, and will become mandatory in September 1999. Another example is the Working Time directive, begun as a partially voluntary measure in 1996 and which becomes mandatory in November 2003. Moreover, managers responsible for paying employees must cope with a major change in modes of payment—from exclusive use of national currency to use of regional currency. From 1999 to 2002, countries with inflation rates low enough to qualify will begin conducting trade using the Euro currency.

These two Europe-wide initiatives are unfolding in countries that already have long and deep traditions of government involvement in setting employee management practices. As mentioned earlier, Switzerland, Luxembourg, and the United Kingdom rank among the fully free economies in the world. But other EU members rank only as mostly free, in the following order (with the most free first): Ireland, Belgium, Austria, Netherlands, Denmark, Finland, Germany, Norway, Sweden, France, Italy, and Spain. All of these countries give government a significant role in influencing personnel practices, with laws restricting layoffs and preserving jobs and/or pay. For example, in recent years, the government of the Netherlands has imposed a freeze on salary increases. Such laws obviously limit managers' flexibility in managing human capital. On the other hand, the EC has not developed any laws against age discrimination, an area of considerable development in the United States—our next focus.

THE NORTH AMERICAN OUTLOOK (U.S. FOCUS)

Free trade among the three nations of North America—Mexico, the United States, and Canada—has been a success by every measure. The growing prosperity of the United States has affected its neighbors, who have in turn contributed to it.

As we go to press, the U.S. economy—the largest in North America—is enjoying a golden age of prosperity. Inflation, interest rates, and unemployment are all at historic lows, while stock values, hiring rates, and capital expenditures are at or near historic highs. (See Box 2-2.) Not surprisingly, business optimism is soaring—that is the firm verdict of ten small-business confidence indicators tracked by the National Federation of Independent Businesses (NFIB) in Washington, D.C.

Small-business owners' plans to hire more employees are at a twenty-five-year high, reports NFIB's November 1997 survey of small businesses. Small-business owners are creating more jobs, and 20 percent plan to expand employment, according to the survey, but a significant number—17 percent—say that their number-one problem is finding qualified labor.

From the point of view of national policymakers, labor shortages seem like good news. They mean fewer drawdowns on government entitlement programs and better results at the polls for incumbents. But

---

BOX 2-2
A Golden Moment: Snapshot of the U.S. Economy in March 1998

Inflation rates	2.3 percent
Interest rates (prime)	7.5 percent
Unemployment rate	4.7 percent (near a 25-year low)
Dow Jones Industrial Average	Hovering around 9,000
Hiring plans	up (20 percent plan to hire, a 25-year high)
Business optimism	high

Sources: Associated Press, National Federation of Independent Businesses, U.S. Department of Labor—all figures from 1998 reports available on the Internet.

---

from the point of view of the businesses themselves, a labor shortage is a real problem—one that will increase over time due to known demographic trends and existing policies and practices.

The silver lining of low unemployment rates has a cloud around it—not of raw labor (people are plentiful) but of skilled labor. And furthermore, even with skilled labor there might be a shortage of human capital—labor that is not only skilled but well managed. The greatest risk faced by economies worldwide may not be unemployment rates, then, but rather *underemployment* rates—a failure to turn human resources into human capital.

A single example will help make this point: The year 2000 problem, which stems from a common limitation in computer programming affecting both software and hardware, is the tendency to recognize only the last two digits of a date field, assuming that the first two digits of any given year must be 19 in all cases—thus, for example, reading 2000 as 1900. Today, nearly two-thirds of all dollars spent in the $114 billion consulting business are devoted to work in information technology, where scarcity of year 2000 expertise is driving prices skyward.

How did this "millennium bug" come to land on our world like a plague of locusts? Was it a lack of strategic planning? No doubt. An absence of total quality management? Possibly. A failure to rise to the reengineering problem? Perhaps. But most of all, it was a woeful *lack of effective human capital management.*

Los Angeles attorney Vito Peraino, a prominent year 2000 doom-sayer writing in the February 1998 issue of *Director's Monthly,* blames the intractability of the year 2000 bug in part on poor human resources planning.

> The problem appears to be worsening not only due to a lack of awareness and commitment by business and an insufficient commitment of resources, but also due to a severe shortage of qualified technicians to address this problem. The Gartner Group, one of the nation's leading computer consultants, estimates that the world is short at least 300,000 programmers to address this problem. This acute shortage has manifested itself in the U.S. by severe upward wage pressure and predatory employment raids by organizations in need of qualified personnel.

Could such critical labor shortages emerge in other sectors? Behind the year 2000 problem in the realm of technology is there a longer-term "year 2020" problem in the larger realm of human capital?

Aside from human capital shortages, there is also the potential problem of overcapacity. Optimism can drive businesses to grow too fast, they say. Companies may take on too much debt, buy too much equipment, hire too many people, and produce too many goods or services, these economists warn. Suppose no one buys the goods and services that are produced, what then? The history of economic cycles since ancient times seems to indicate that what goes up must come down—often with a crash.

Wall Street Journal veteran Bernard Wysocki, Jr., reporting on a high level of U.S. business confidence in early 1998, dutifully includes early warnings about the dangers of extreme optimism. He quotes Sherman Roberts of Harvard University's John F. Kennedy School of Government on "overly optimistic decisionmaking," and Edgar Peters of Panagora Asset Management in Boston on unseen hazards ahead—the U.S. economy may be a supertanker but could end up like the "Exxon *Valdez.*"

Yet even while noting the importance of a healthy dose of negative thinking, Wysocki—who has served with distinction as bureau chief for the *Journal* in several major U.S. cities—puts his sterling reputation on the line by proposing the highly unconventional idea that *it may be possible to sustain prosperity indefinitely if companies as a group can maintain high levels of employment.*

Wysocki's extraordinary observation has obvious relevance to the topic of human capital, so we quote it at some length.

> It is difficult, however, to see where business "'pessimism" would come from today. Economists have long held that business confidence mostly reflects consumer confidence and consumer behavior and that, in turn, consumers' high spirits derive mostly from the job market, which is clearly superb.
>
> A large and rising percentage of Americans say jobs are plentiful. Why not? The slow recovery of the early 1990s, when new jobs were scarce, is long past. Today, the economy is creating well over 200,000 jobs a month, and, in some months, the net new-job figure tops 300,000. . . . The flip side of strong job growth, of course, is a low unemployment rate. To some economists, this is a Rosetta stone of sorts, the key to unlocking the mystery of "animal spirits."

Could it be that the U.S. economy has indeed found this Rosetta stone—a sustainably high rate of employment based on good employment practices? This possibility was foreshadowed in the Hudson Institute's landmark study *Workforce 2000: Work and Workers for the 21st Century,* by William B. Johnston and Arnold H. Packer, published by the Indianapolis-based Hudson Institute in 1987. This study, funded primarily by the U.S. Department of Labor, looked to the future and predicted major changes in the nation's human capital. (Dave Walker, one of the authors of this book, was an assistant secretary of labor and participated in this effort, which was championed by former labor secretary, Bill Brock.)

- First, *Workforce 2000* predicted that the U.S. economy would grow at a healthy pace, fueled by a rebound in U.S. exports, productivity growth, and a strong world economy.
- Second, this clairvoyant study foresaw that because of productivity gains in manufacturing, job growth would come from the service sector.

- Third, the study rightly predicted a need for increased skills by workers newly entering the workforce. Because of the growth in technology, and of the service sector in general, the workers of tomorrow would need strong reading and mathematics skills.
- Finally, *Workforce 2000* drew a prescient picture of the future workforce, declaring that it would grow slowly, and contain a higher percentage of older, female, minority, and/or immigrant workers.

Workforce 2000 advised policymakers and managers alike to take action on six fronts:

- Advance the cause of free trade.
- Improve productivity in service industries.
- Improve dynamism of the aging workforce.
- Reconcile the needs of women, work, and families.
- Integrate Blacks and Hispanics fully into the workforce.
- Improve workers' educations and skills.

Policies, said the authors, can make a difference. They warned against attempts to hold back the pace of change and cling to an old industrial structure. These attempts, they said, could damage the economy:

> On the other hand, the policies that appear to take risks by pushing the limits of growth, accelerating investment in *human* and physical *capital,* and removing the institutional barriers to productivity enhancements in services, can pay huge dividends. [Emphasis added.]

So what happened? In *Workforce 2020: Work and Workers in the 21ˢᵗ Century* (1997), by Richard W. Judy and Carol d'Amico, a sequel to *Workforce 2000*, we learn that the four main predictions came true.

- Today, in comparison to a decade ago, U.S. exports have doubled (to $584 billion at last count), and U.S. gross domestic products have increased by nearly a quarter (to $7 trillion at last count).
- Although manufacturing productivity ("value added") has risen by 36 percent since 1987, the number of manufacturing jobs has held steady. All new job growth has come from the service sector.
- The skill level of new service jobs is increasingly high, as predicted.

- In the past decade, the U.S. civilian workforce has grown by only thirteen million, with women and minorities making the greatest net gains in employment.

In sum, the Hudson Institute economists were right when they tried to peer into the future over ten years ago. So what do they see on the horizon for human capital over the next two decades? Here are the top four predictions featured in *Workforce 2020:*

- First, *Workforce 2020* predicts that increasing technological change will result in net job growth. Although technological advances will automate many jobs or shift them to lower-paid workers in other countries, this negative will be offset by a positive: a job boom in the development, marketing, and servicing of this newly sophisticated technology. This boom will be enhanced by the business improvements that this technology generates. The net result will be job growth—and even labor shortages. These new jobs based in advanced technology will be indifferent to location, nationality, gender, race, and age, leading to a broader distribution of employment among all geographic and demographic groups. Much job growth will be in part-time and contract work rather than full-time employment.

- Second, the new study anticipates that the global economy will affect U.S. businesses more than ever before. The percentage of manufacturing jobs that depend on exports will grow from its current level of 20 percent. These will tend to be highly skilled and highly paid. On the other hand, low-skilled jobs in the United States will become scarce and will pay very low wages. Employment growth will remain concentrated in the service sector, which will also benefit from export markets. Volatility in many market sectors will give a strong advantage to small businesses.

- Third, the new study expects continued aging of the U.S. workforce. By 2020, notes the study, almost 20 percent of the U.S. population will be sixty-five or older, notes the study. Some will retire, creating job openings for younger workers. Many will not, bringing maturity to the American workforce. In either event, these older citizens will become an important market for businesses. (To realize the enormity of the trend, consider the fact that in 1950, when Social Security began,

there were 16 workers for every retired person in the United States, and today the ratio is 3.3 workers per retiree.)
- And finally, *Workforce 2020* predicts continued diversification of the workforce, especially with regard to ethnicity. Whereas today, workers of European ancestry hold 76 percent of all jobs, their share of jobs will drop to 68 percent by 2020. The balance will be filled with Hispanics (rising to 14 percent from 9 percent in this decade), African-Americans (holding steady at 11 percent), and Asians (rising to 6 percent from 3 percent).

Taken together, these four new trends bode well for the future of human capital in America—and potentially throughout North America and beyond, where similar trends are occurring. Even in Southeast Asia, once reputed to have a relatively young population, policymakers are addressing the question of an aging workforce. The International Monetary Fund has even published a paper recently entitled "Aging in the Asian Tigers: Challenges for Fiscal Policy." Companies will have more high-skill jobs to offer, and these jobs will be performed by an older, more diverse pool of employees. Companies can turn these human resources into human capital if managers are free to manage—and use that freedom to manage globally.

CONCLUSION

The mosaic we have presented here forms part of a larger, shifting pattern. The economic conditions we describe may change before this book comes to market—and these conditions will surely continue to change in the coming months and years. Yet a close look at the evanescent issues captured here can be instructive, because each situation described could happen to any country sooner or later.

Every nation bears the risk of sudden financial crisis and rising unemployment—the conditions that several countries in Asia are experiencing as we go to press. Every nation copes with changes in its legal and monetary infrastructure, just as Europe must do today.

And every nation wants to learn how to hold on to prosperity—the enviable task for the United States at this fleeting moment.

Moreover, these differing conditions all require the same focus on fundamentals. Whether managers are called to recover from crisis, to respond to change, or to sustain growth, they need the freedom to build the primary wealth of their companies: human capital. The remainder of this book presents a model for doing just that.

Chapter Three

HUMAN CAPITAL APPRAISAL™

A Five-Squared Approach

> Like the gyroscope's fall,
> truly unequivocal
> because trued by regnant certainty,
>
> it is a power of
> strong enchantment.

—Marianne Moore, "The Mind is an Enchanting Thing"

Every company wants to realize a return on its assets. Why not a return on its investment in human capital? And if so, how? Charismatic leaders come and go, and positive climates perish. The incentive program that inspires excellence in one company may drag down another, and a culture that ensures survival in one market may hasten failure in another. Problems of compliance, communication, and technology can surface at any time, erasing hard-won achievements.

Just as success in the marketplace cannot be based on any one strategy, so success in the management of human capital cannot be based on any one factor. Instead, it can be achieved only through proper methodology—a company's stage-by-stage, factor-by-factor, conscious, committed approach to the measurement, management, and leveraging of its human capital. This methodology must be, in the words of poet Marianne Moore, "trued by regnant certainty"—that is, it must be grounded in objective facts. At the same time, it must have, to quote Moore again, a "power of strong enchantment" based on its appeal to people's hearts and minds.

Having a methodology to manage human capital goes far beyond having a budget and staff for human resources. Most companies have human resources personnel and various HR policies and programs, but few companies know their value—or how to enhance it. In the view of too many corporate chiefs, HR managers are mere functionaries implementing programs that are no more than extra costs to be cut in times of trouble. Indeed, it is a well-documented fact that in economic downturns, training budgets take the quickest and deepest cuts.

Everyone in progressive organizations recognizes that the HR function must become more closely linked to strategy. As the HR function evolves from administrative to strategic, the question can be asked (and objectively answered), what are we doing to enhance the value of human capital in our organization? Although the effectiveness of the HR department is a part of this answer, it is only one part. Arthur Andersen has developed an approach that can help companies measure the value of all policies affecting human capital, and align these policies more closely to corporate goals. This method, which we call Human Capital Appraisal™, shows how companies can *measure and increase the returns on their investments in people.*

We believe that there are a series of necessary stages in the management of human capital, and that within *each* stage *all* the major human capital factors must be covered. In this chapter, we will give an overview of the main stages and areas of the human capital appraisal process, with more detailed guidance to follow in the next five chapters.

THE FIVE STAGES OF HUMAN CAPITAL APPRAISAL

"To everything there is a season, and a time to every purpose under the heaven," wrote the anonymous author of the biblical text Ecclesiastes. This phrase, set to music in our generation by the Byrds rock group, is true not only of life, but also of human capital management. Any manager seeking to improve returns on human capital in a company must begin at the beginning and move forward stage by stage.

Stage One: Clarification

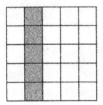

Companies seeking to improve their returns on human capital must begin at the beginning, with what we call *clarification*. In this stage, a company identifies and confirms its overall business direction or strategy in the broadest sense of the terms. This assessment looks at the company's business goals, its overall culture and values, and its management philosophy—and then it assesses the impact of these on human capital. Chapter 4 will explore this important phase.

Stage Two: Assessment

The next stage follows from the last and sets the stage for all the others. It is the all-important phase we call *assessment*. In this phase, companies calculate the cost of investment in human capital, and the value employees place on this investment. An important part of this stage is the calibration of strategic and operational "fit," using known best practices as an operational benchmark. In Chapter 5, we will explore the assessment phase more fully.

Stage Three: Design

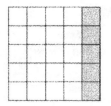

In the *design* stage, companies begin to create programs that can yield better returns on human capital. Design is the moment of creativity for the firm, working with its advisers. We will take a closer look at the design phase of human capital enhancement in Chapter 6.

Stage Four: Implementation

In the *implementation* stage, companies put these proposed changes into practice. Without implementation, ideas are devoid of meaning. As William James said, "Truth happens to an idea. It *becomes* true, is *made* true by events." It is actions, not words, that will tell if a company is "lying" when it says it values human resources—as we shall see in Chapter 7.

Stage Five: Monitoring

Finally, in the *monitoring* stage, the new system must be checked against strategy. This is the true test of the Human Capital Appraisal™

approach. The purpose of making changes, after all, is to improve the fit between the company's strategy and its human capital programs. In this monitoring stage, a company needs to check that the intended changes are indeed happening. It is in the monitoring stage that the actual improvements can be measured and quantified.

In the event that things are not turning out as planned, a company then can pinpoint where the problem is. Is it in the plan itself, or is it in an area such as compliance or communication? By checking the implementation of all the areas against strategic objectives and key performance indicators, companies can identify and resolve problems. Chapter 8 will guide readers through this process.

THE FIVE AREAS OF HUMAN CAPITAL MANAGEMENT

During all five stages, companies need to look at all five areas of human capital. The first, as mentioned, is *recruitment, retention, and retirement.*

The second is the closely related area of *rewards and performance management.*

Next comes *career development, succession planning, and training.*

A fourth area is *organizational structure.*

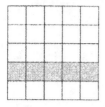

The fifth and final area requiring management attention, as mentioned, is the broad realm of what might be called *human capital enablers*—systems for improving legal compliance, employee and industrial relations, communications, and information flow.

Like the facets of a diamond, these areas will change in color depending on how they are held to the light. The clarification process will help companies see all these areas as extensions of strategy. Assessment will yield yet another perspective on the areas, as will the equally important stages of design, implementation, and monitoring.

There is no real magic in the number 5 or in the squaring. Given the richness of English (or any modern language), this model could be reconfigured into a greater or lesser number of elements in either dimension. What matters most in this approach (or in any similar model) is the completeness and integration of the elements. Our experience tells us—and our clients confirm—that companies must pass through certain stages and manage certain elements, and that these stages and elements, however they are labeled, must be integrated. That is, there must be a multiplication effect that integrates the phases with the factors—hence our grid:

A CLOSER LOOK

The process of human capital appraisal is infinitely complex, yet it is manageable. Visualizing this process as five stages and five areas can

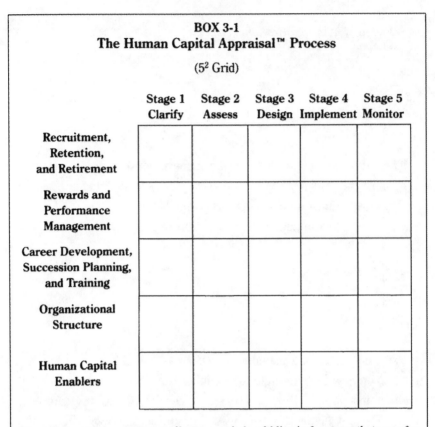

BOX 3-1
The Human Capital Appraisal™ Process

(5² Grid)

	Stage 1 Clarify	Stage 2 Assess	Stage 3 Design	Stage 4 Implement	Stage 5 Monitor
Recruitment, Retention, and Retirement					
Rewards and Performance Management					
Career Development, Succession Planning, and Training					
Organizational Structure					
Human Capital Enablers					

The grid shows the management of human capital unfolding in five stages that cover five broad factors or "areas" in the management of human capital—hence our term 5².

help managers move through it with speed and thoroughness. In the following five chapters, we will be taking a look, stage by stage, at each of these areas.

Models must be useful as well as truthful, and simplicity is often associated with both qualities. It is well-known in information circles that there is a limit to the amount of information that human beings can process. In fact, seven items (give or take) seems to be the limit. Our model, with five dimensions and five stages, errs on the side of simplicity. In the words of Marianne Moore, we believe that the rigor of this model makes it "trued by regnant certainty." We also hope that it rings true to those who use it, granting the model and the managers who use it a "power of strong enchantment."

CONCLUSION

Human Capital Appraisal™ is a holistic approach based on the two equally important dimensions of stages and areas—time and space. It is in the squaring of these elements that the real substance of human capital development can emerge. By following a sequence for enhancing human capital, and by ensuring coverage of all areas within each part of the sequence, companies can improve their returns on investment in this area—by far the most critical for companies today.

Chapter Four

CLARIFICATION

Defining the People Impact of Business Strategy

> We must learn to explore all the options and possibilities
> that confront us in a changing world.
>
> —James William Fulbright, *speech in the U.S. Senate*

A s business leaders plan for the future, they assume an awesome responsibility. At this turn of the millennium, more than in any past era, the goals leaders set, the timing they choose, and the resources they commit can have a "life or death" impact on their businesses. In today's winner-take-all environment, company plans are disclosed more fully, judged more harshly, and tested more quickly than in the past. Rapidly changing technology ensures that competitive advantage lasts no more than "a nanosecond," in the words of Bill Gates. Yet today more than ever, shareholders and other stakeholders demand accountability to the future as well as to the present.

At the same time, today's business leaders have a new secret weapon for planning—if they choose to use it. That secret weapon is the concept of human capital. In the aftermath of excessive downsizing, many companies are beginning to see the vital connection between people and value. People, companies are discovering, are not merely an "expense" on the income statement but an "asset" hidden off the balance sheet— an asset that not only adds value but also ensures the organization's very survival. Later in this book (Chapter 11), we will explore the accounting and financial implications of this discovery. This chapter takes a more immediate look, beginning at the all-important starting point of *strategic planning* and its link to human capital.

Why should companies try to link human capital plans to business strategy? The answer is very simple. Without such a link, the business strategy may not be achieved. If the strategy is not achieved, the business may fail, and all the employees could lose their jobs—starting first and foremost with the director of human resources!

For several years now, there have been a rash of articles declaring the end of the HR director position as we now know it. Many of them have made a clarion call for change in this area—a change from mere personnel functions to a high-level strategic environment.

Human Resource Management Journal has published scholarly research on this topic, including a recent British article featuring case studies from a health care company and an electronics company. The article concludes that there is indeed a shift toward a more strategic use of the HR function, and that companies making this shift are experiencing success:

> While it would be unwise to make sweeping prescriptions upon the slender base of these two case studies, the findings we have reported seem to be indicative of a shift toward the more strategic use of HR initiatives, with encouraging business outcomes for those organisations who adopt such an approach. . . . What we have elaborated here are some of the important linkages between an organisation's strategic purposes on the one hand, and the practicalities of implementing HR practices on the other.

This and many other publications make it abundantly clear that the HR director's job is changing. Clearly, HR directors must find a way to link their work to the strategic objectives of their organizations. Conversely, and more importantly, *directors and senior managers must link their planning work to existing and future programs for human capital.* Companies and other organizations need strategic clarification for their human capital programs.

So much for the "why" of strategic clarification. The truly pressing issue now becomes how: By what means can senior managers and others link strategy to human capital programs?

WHY CLARIFY?

As explained in the previous chapter, the enhancement of human capital must progress in stages—from clarification, to appraisal, to design, to implementation, and to monitoring. In this chapter, we shall explain more about the clarification stage, in which managers examine their human capital programs to ensure that they fit the organization's overall strategy and culture.

The need for clarification in this sense is great. Traditionally in larger companies the planning and people aspects of business have been separated into two worlds. The world of planning has been reserved for the "mahogany row" of senior management and the board, while the world of people has unfolded a few floors down, in the department of human resources.

All too often these two worlds have worked at cross-purposes. The board may approve a bold new strategic plan from a new CEO, and expect the director of human resources (HR) to continue implementing the same evaluation and compensation policies—even if the plan and the policies clash. (For example, the strategic plan might seek to lower customer turnover, but the compensation plan might not include any incentives to retain old customers—only to attract new ones.) Conversely, an HR director might initiate a change that clashes with company strategy or vision. (For example, the HR director might decide to eliminate a popular low-cost health benefit tied in with a local hospital at precisely the time that the board of directors has made community relations a top priority.)

Compensation is not the only human capital area that can conflict with strategy. In the area of training, a company may spend large amounts of money teaching the employees a new skill that works against company goals. For example, at a major British bank, tellers were generously rewarded for higher cash accuracy during transactions at their windows. The new incentive system increased the accuracy of counts for teller drawers, but it led to long lines and, eventually, customer defections.

Further fragmentation occurs within the HR function, where various initiatives can proceed independently of each other—a pay plan here, a performance appraisal process there, a broadbanding program over there.

At best, such a disconnect between planning and the HR function (not to mention disconnects within the HR function) can slow progress. At worst, they can prevent it. Why? Because the planning function and the human capital function are inextricably linked. So the question for senior and other managers is not whether to align the two; it is how to do so. Therefore, the first stage in our Human Capital Appraisal™ model requires attentive consideration to the organization's current strategy—in the broadest sense of the term—and an analysis of how that strategy is affecting human capital in the organization. We will begin with an overview, and then get to specifics.

CLARIFYING HUMAN CAPITAL APPRAISAL (FIVE AREAS)

As mentioned, any effort to enhance the value of human capital in a company or other organization must begin with a broad view, or clarification (Stage 1). The purpose of this stage in the human capital enhancement process is to assess and scope business context and HR issues while beginning a companywide communication and involvement process.

Early communication allows the company's human capital review to be positioned correctly with employees while seeking and feeding back their opinions on matters that affect them. The aim is to involve the entire organization in contributing opinions on a broad range of cultural and human capital questions to identify key issues and priorities. This feedback contributes to an overall appraisal of human capital policies (Stage 2), which in turn may lead to the design of new policies (Stage 3), implementation of those policies (Stage 4), and, finally, an ongoing effort to ensure that the policies align with the company's intended strategy (Stage 5).

As mentioned in the previous chapter, we have grouped the many aspects of human capital into five general areas:

• Recruitment, retention, and retirement.
• Performance management and rewards (including retirement pay).

- Career development, succession planning, and training.
- Organizational structure.
- Human capital enablers.

From the outset, every business strategy must be examined against these elements. Of course, no two programs for recruitment, rewards, or training are exactly alike. Overall company structure will vary, as will various processes for compliance and communication. The following discussion is offered as a very general checklist that senior executives and human resources managers alike can use to link the two worlds of strategy and people. The model presented in this chapter can help human capital managers to think along planning lines while they manage, as well as to help senior managers and directors to think along human capital lines while they plan. Now for the specifics.

Clarification of Recruitment, Retention, and Retirement

When assessing the impact of a given strategy on human capital, one vital question—and for many organizations the natural first question—concerns the "body count" the strategy will entail. In other words, managers need to assess how the strategy will affect the coming and going of people, and, most important, the retention of key people. Here is a brief checklist that can apply to almost any strategy.

- *Recruitment.* What is the current system for recruitment in the company? Is it adequate? How many openings are there in the company now for what positions? How many openings are anticipated over the next five years, and for what positions? What are the marketplace demographics for those positions? How long does it take the company to recruit? Will an executive search firm be retained to find the needed talent? How will bringing in new talent affect existing talent? Does the new talent bring needed competencies and qualifications?

- *Retention.* What programs now exist for employee retention? Are they sufficient? Will the new strategy make it more difficult to retain key people? Have they been consulted for their views on the strategy?

- *Retirement.* What is the current retirement policy at the company? Is it appropriate given current and expected market demographics and trends in available labor force, workforce composition, regulatory policies, and related arenas? Is it flexible? How will the new strategy affect retirement programs? Will it require early retirement by a significant number of executives or skilled workers? What will the accounting charge be for this early retirement program? What is the relationship between current and deferred compensation?

Clarification of Performance Management and Rewards

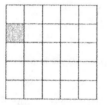

- *Performance management.* What is the current status of performance management in the company? How effective is it? Beyond pay incentives, does the new strategy include other incentives for performance? Will the new strategy cause changes in the way performance is being managed? What do managers and other employees think of these changes? Is performance management linked with succession planning and training and development? Is it viewed as credible in the organization? How effective are existing competency models in changing behaviors?

- *Rewards.* What is the current system for rewards in the company? Is it linked to the enterprise's strategy? Does it work effectively, or could it be improved? Was the board of directors and/or the board compensation committee involved in shaping the pay strategy? At

what level—senior management only, or throughout the organization? Is the compensation and benefits plan for senior managers only,
or does it extend to middle managers and others? How is the pay plan
perceived by employees at all levels? Are pay and performance linked
at the employee level? Senior management level? Board level? Is it
linked to shareholder interests?

Clarification of Career Development, Succession Planning, and Training

· *Career development.* What is the current system for career development in the company? Does it work well? Will the new strategy trigger changes in the lines of reporting within the organization? If so,
how will it change the existing paths for career development? How
will these changes be perceived—as opportunities or threats? What
can senior management do to ensure a positive impact for its most
motivated employees?

· *Succession planning.* What is the current system for succession planning in the company? Do succession plans exist for all key roles and
critical skilled positions? Is there an emergency succession plan for
these roles, in the event of a sudden loss through abrupt resignation,
illness, or death?

· *Training.* What is the current investment environment for training in
the company? How are individual training needs identified? Do managers and other employees find the programs relevant to their needs?
Will the new strategy require an increase in training? In what areas?
Will these be provided internally, or will outside trainers be engaged?
How are training programs developed and delivered in the organization? Is the training supplemented by managerial coaching? Peer
coaching? Self-coaching? (See next point.)

Clarification of Organizational Structure

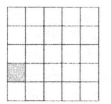

- *Outsourcing/insourcing.* What is the company's current balance between internal and external providers of support services? Is this balance satisfactory for managers and other employees? Will the new strategy change this balance? In what areas? More generally, will the company's strategy require people to work together in a new way? If so, how will this new way affect the insource/outsource balance? Is the company moving toward or away from the heavily outsourced "virtual company" model? Are outsource service providers achieving quality service standards over time?
- *Effectiveness of the human resources function.* What level of human resources support staff does the company now have? How effective does it seem to managers and other employees? How will the new strategy affect this function? Are HR functions clearly understood in the organization?

Clarification of HR Enablers

- *Legal and accounting compliance.* What is the current compliance profile for the company with respect to human capital? How is the company's record on this score perceived by those inside the company (managers and other employees) and outside the company (stockholders, customers, and other employees)? Will the new strategy mitigate any risks in this area? Will it increase any risks? How does management plan to manage these changes?

- *Employee and industrial relations.* Overall, what is the state of employee and industrial (labor) relations in the company? Will the new strategy change the tenor of relations? In what way? How can managers steer relations in a positive direction as the strategy unfolds?
- *Communications.* How are communications currently facilitated at the company? How do managers and other employees perceive the effectiveness and integrity of the company's current "communications culture"? How will the new strategy affect communications? What will managers do to ensure positive, open communications throughout the period of change ahead? Is the communications function being used to help employees understand and appreciate human capital programs?
- *Human capital information systems and other systems.* What kind of information technology is currently supporting the company's human capital managers? How will the new strategy affect this information system? Also, how can the information system be used to support the new strategy? Does the system need changing? Do other systems need changing?

The answers to these questions require in-depth surveys of managers and employees. In Appendix A, at the end of this book, we provide a case study of clarification surveys we conducted at a client company, including sample survey questions and scores.

CONCLUSION

Planning and people issues have been separated in too many companies. The two can and should be linked through a process we call clarification. This is the first and most critical stage of human capital enhancement. It links current and future human capital programs to the overall business strategy and culture of a company. This process depends greatly on communication and commitment, and relies on surveys and face-to-face interviews to ensure both.

Chapter Five

ASSESSMENT

Measuring the Fit, Cost, and Value
of Current Human Capital Programs

> They wonder much to hear that gold, which in itself is so
> useless a thing, should be everywhere so much esteemed,
> that even men for whom it was made, and by whom it has
> its value, should yet be thought of less value than it is.

—Sir Thomas More, *Utopia* (1516)

The managers of human capital today must be visionary, but what is vision? Most managers think of this trait as farsightedness—the ability to see the long-term view and the big picture. But when it comes to human capital, true vision requires a close look as well.

True, managers must begin the human capital appraisal process with a look at the far horizon—as they seek to grasp the general direction of their company's human capital programs and how those programs fit with the company's strategy and culture. Equally important, however, is the ability to see very clearly and concretely the components *within* the big picture. To manage human capital effectively, managers must master the very rigorous science of *assessment*—the second stage in the human capital appraisal process.

This chapter will explore this important flip side of human capital vision—close attention to the specific components of human capital in an organization. In our view, assessment means more than inventorying costs, although it certainly includes this activity. And assessment is more than a matter of cutting costs, although it may well trigger this result. To be complete, the human capital appraisal process requires careful measurement of the fit, the cost, and—most important—the value of all current human capital programs in a company. Some companies may already be making these assessments, but rarely do companies make them jointly. Later on in this chapter, we will introduce a tool, called the Fit-Cost-Value™ matrix, that can help managers do this.

ASSESSING HUMAN CAPITAL

By the time managers are ready for the assessment stage, they will already have a general sense of how well various human capital programs may fit the company's strategy. But their early work in strategic clarification gave them only a macro view. Assessment involves a closer, micro look at each program's precise fit with strategy, and careful measurement of costs in relation to value as well. This requires asking and answering a series of questions about fit, cost, and value in all the human capital areas—from basic issues such as recruitment to enablers such as information systems.

Fit Recap

The first question will be a general recap question covering the strategic fit of programs in the particular area. Ideally, companies will already know the answer to this question for each area as a result of the clarification stage. This answer is basically a carryover from the clarification stage.

We saw in the previous chapter that a big-picture review of fit must be based on interviews with senior managers, employees, and stakeholders. At the assessment stage, interviews continue, this time focusing initially on costs. Key interviewees here are human resources managers, operational managers, and financial staff.

In the assessment stage, managers need to link fit concerns to the equally important concerns of cost and value. In this deeper look at fit, managers may also look at how well the programs fit the programs of benchmark companies, and at how the programs fit market practices. We will discuss this in greater detail in Chapter 9.

Cost Analysis

In analyzing the costs of a human capital program, managers must be thorough—and demand thoroughness of their analysts. A full cost analysis will include:

- The *direct costs* of each program, including the costs of facilities, outside providers, and systems, as well as the fixed and variable out-of-pocket hard costs.
- The *indirect costs* created as a result of the program, such as the tax consequences of certain forms of retirement savings plans.
- The *opportunity costs* of each program, such as time employees spend away from their jobs because of the program, or the time managers spend making it happen.

Costs can be broken down by business unit, function, and other parameters, as well as by specific programs. A cost-per-employee measurement can be used to assess human capital costs against competitor and "best practices" data. The head count figure in the cost-per-employee ratio should be adjusted to reflect the use of nonemployees such as consultants and contractors, and leased, part-time, and/or temporary employees. (For more on this subject, see Chapter 10.)

Value Added

For each cost measurement of the program, managers need to analyze benefits realized as value added to human capital. This analysis will focus on various impacts, including the impacts of:

- pay on performance;
- benefits on retention/morale;
- training on productivity;
- performance review on career development and succession planning;
- the employee assistance plan on staff turnover.

As a part of this assessment, management can survey employees (through written surveys, interviews, and/or focus groups) to find out the relative values they place on particular programs. Properly conducted, this analysis reveals not only such general attitudes as "satisfaction with benefits," but also specific perceptions about which benefits are most important to the employee as part of total compensation and which are unappreciated or undervalued. Similar value-added assessment exercises can be performed in connection with operational managers and HR managers. All of these assessment exercises can help to identify existing "expectation gaps" that require management attention and action.

THE FIT-COST-VALUE™ MATRIX

Each human capital program or activity can be positioned on a Fit-Cost-Value™ matrix. By plotting all of these results together on a matrix, companies can begin to see the full human capital picture in their organizations. Box 5-1 shows how a particular company might plot the fit, cost, and value of its human capital programs. In this particular case, the company was studying nine separate human capital programs, so there are nine entries on the matrix.

This sample company (a composite based on our work) saw the following results, starting from the southeast quadrant and moving clockwise:

- One of the programs (shown in the southwest quadrant) has a low strategic fit and a high cost in relation to value.
  Action: Replace—or cut altogether.
- Three of the programs (shown in the northwest quadrant) have a high strategic fit and a high cost in relation to value.
  Action: Improve cost/value balance. (Look back at cost and value to understand what needs to change.)
- Four of the programs (shown in the northeast quadrant) have a high strategic fit and a low cost in relation to value.
  Action: Maintain and improve.
- Two of the programs (shown in the southeast quadrant) have a low strategic fit and a low cost in relation to value.
  Action: Align with strategy.

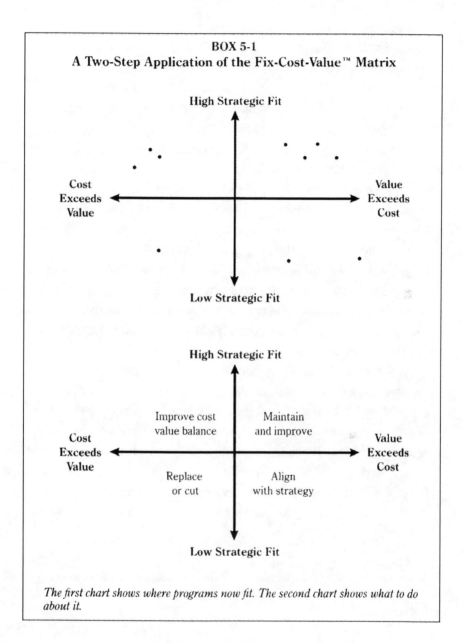

BOX 5-1
A Two-Step Application of the Fix-Cost-Value™ Matrix

The first chart shows where programs now fit. The second chart shows what to do about it.

AN ASSESSMENT CHECKLIST

The following human capital assessment checklist offers a hands-on, operational approach. Like all the checklists in this book, it covers the five main areas of human capital management.

The checklist in the previous chapter showed how the five human capital areas link to or *fit* general strategic concerns. The checklist in the present chapter carries over this fit component. It also seeks knowledge on cost, and uses the information on both to determine value.

We have created individual fit-cost-value checklists for each area of human capital management. Because the same basic fit-cost-value process must be used to assess all human capital areas, readers may think it would be better to have a single checklist for all areas, instead of many small ones that are similar and therefore repetitious. Our purpose is twofold. First, a generic checklist would be less useful when assessing a specific area. Second, needs vary by area. For example, some areas—such as recruitment, retention, and non-pay aspects of retirement—have low and/or variable costs that do not lend themselves to detailed ratio analysis. By contrast, the area of rewards has a high fixed cost that demands such analysis. For most effective use, readers should glance over all the lists to see their range, reading them closely only when using a particular list.

Each area has its own "red flag" list based on Arthur Andersen's extensive fieldwork and research in this area. (For research sources, see the Bibliography.) This part of the checklist calls management's attention to problem areas that often come up for companies during the assessment process. In these trouble spots, typically fit is low and/or cost is high, leading to an overall low value. Some of the red flags can be seen in employee attitude surveys, others must be derived from looking at the numbers—or simply keeping in touch with the grapevine of common wisdom.

Assessment of Programs for Recruitment, Retention, and Retirement

- *Recruitment.* Based on the findings of the initial clarification process, how do current recruitment programs fit the company's strategy and culture with respect to senior managers, employees, and key stake-holders? What is the total cost of the current recruitment process (including direct, indirect, and opportunity costs)? For example, how much is the company paying for executive recruiters, sign-on bonuses, and employment advertising? How do these costs break down by unit? By function? By program? What is the cost per employee? How do recruitment costs compare to benchmark, best practices, and competitor costs? Are these costs growing? How fast? Having measured these costs, how do they stack up in relation to the perceived value of the program?

Bottom line: Plot the fit (high or low) and cost/value ratio (high or low) of recruitment programs on a matrix.

Red flags for recruitment: Patterns of discrimination in recruitment (few or restricted hires of the physically challenged, minorities, older workers, women). Hiring the wrong people (unqualified, unethical). Relying too much on reference letters. Hiring too many people or too few. Creating ill will by taking key players from competitors (head-hunting/body-snatching). Low rate of acceptance for offers of employment. Chronic use of recruitment as a solution to heavy turnover in key positions. High opportunity cost of line managers may signal an ineffective screening process.

- *Retention.* Based on the findings of the initial clarification process, how do current programs for retention *fit* the company's strategy and culture with respect to senior managers, employees, and key stakeholders? What is the *total cost* of the current retention system in the company (including direct, indirect, and opportunity costs)? For example, what is the cost of senior executive "golden handcuff" programs? Are these costs growing? How fast? How do these costs stack up in relation to the perceived *value* of the program?

Bottom line: Plot the fit (high or low) and cost/value ratio (high or low) of retention programs on a matrix.

Red flags for retention: Turnover that is very high, very low, or extremely variable in comparison to benchmarks. Perceptions that the company is keeping the wrong people (see also recruitment) or keeping the right people but putting them in the wrong jobs (see also career development). High employee-to-sales ratio in comparison to benchmarks (may indicate passive rather than active retention). Unacceptable voluntary versus involuntary attrition ratios.

- *Retirement.* Building on the findings of the initial clarification process, how does the timing of current retirement programs *fit* the company's strategy and culture with respect to senior managers, employees, and key stakeholders? What are the extra *costs* of this timing factor over and above the hard costs of retirement pay (covered following under rewards)? For example, are there any pending lawsuits challenging retirement actions based on the policy's timing? How do these costs stack up against the perceived *value* of the program?

  Bottom line: Plot the fit (high or low) and cost/value ratio (high or low) of retirement programs on a matrix.

  Red flags for retirement (see also rewards): No clear retirement policy. A retirement policy that moves people out too early or too late. At board level, use of retirement policies in lieu of evaluation. Regulatory compliance problems or poor employee communications. (See also retirement items under "rewards" category below.)

Assessment of Performance Management and Rewards

- *Performance management.* Based on the findings of the initial clarification process, how do current performance management programs *fit* the company's strategy and culture with respect to senior managers, employees, and key stakeholders? Do performance objectives support the business strategy? Are objectives set for employees at all levels? Are the objectives clear, measurable, achievable, and controllable? What is the *total cost* of the performance management programs (including direct, indirect, and opportunity costs)? For example, what percentage of all senior management time is spent on performance management? Adding up such costs, how do they break down by unit? By function? By program? What is the cost per employee? How do cost ratios compare to benchmark, best practices, and competitor costs? Are these costs growing? How fast? How do these costs stack up against the perceived *value* of these programs?

Bottom line: Plot the fit (high or low) and cost/value ratio (high or low) of performance management programs on a matrix.

Red flags for performance management: Line management burnout. Customer complaints about "apathetic" or, conversely, "aggressive" employees. Requests for transfers. Low productivity. Cynicism or indifference to performance management on the part of employees who are managing and/or employees being managed. Development of competencies not aligned with fundamental business needs. Slow cycle time (in manufacturing).

• *Rewards.* Based on the findings of the initial clarification process, how do current pay programs *fit* the company's strategy and culture with respect to senior managers, employees, and key stakeholders? What is the *total cost* of the current rewards system (including direct, indirect, and opportunity costs)? What are the costs for the basic units of pay: salary, bonuses, incentive pay, and benefits? How are benefits apportioned among medical, retirement, and perquisites? How do these various costs break down by unit? By function? By program? What is the cost per employee? Per revenues? Per income? How do pay ratios compare to benchmark, best practices, and competitor costs? Are costs growing? How fast? How do costs stack up to perceived *value* of pay programs?

Bottom line: Plot the fit (high or low) and cost/value ratio (high or low) of rewards on a matrix.

Red flags for rewards: Pay too high or too low in relation to market benchmarks. No effective link to strategy. Board and senior management focus on gold, not tin—no focus on mid-level salaried or lower-level hourly employees. Employee perception that pay is low and/or unfairly distributed. High proportion of fixed versus variable pay. Negative stock market response to changes in compensation programs (such as a charge for early retirement pay triggered by a restructuring). A proliferation of programs driving costs up with little value delivered. Limited flexibility in the design of employee benefit programs.

Assessment of Career Development, Succession Planning, and Training

- *Career development.* Based on the findings of the initial clarification process, how do current career development programs *fit* the company's strategy and culture with respect to senior managers, employees, and key stakeholders? Are there structural problems impeding career development, such as a strict hierarchy with very few top positions? What is the *total cost* of the career development programs (including direct, indirect, and opportunity costs)? How do these costs stack up against the perceived *value* of the programs?

  Bottom line: Plot the fit (high or low) and cost/value ratio (high or low) of career development programs on a matrix.

  Red flags for career development: High turnover. Habitual use of recruiters to fill newly empty positions. No link to succession planning or training. Low morale. Departing employees saying in their exit interviews that they had no clear career path or programs.

- *Succession planning.* Based on the findings of the initial clarification process, how do current succession planning programs fit the company's strategy and culture with respect to senior managers, employees, and key stakeholders? Are there structural problems impeding succession planning, such as lack of information about talent in lower management levels? What is the total cost of the succession planning system (including direct, indirect, and opportunity costs)? How do these costs stack up against the perceived value of the system?

  Bottom line: Plot the fit (high or low) and cost/value ratio (high or low) of succession planning on a matrix.

  Red flags for succession planning: No formal succession plan for positions other than the CEO position, if that! General complaints (with or without formal plans) about lack of succession planning. No link between succession planning and career development or training.

• *Training.* Based on the findings of the initial clarification process, how do current training programs fit the company's strategy and culture with respect to senior managers, employees, and key stakeholders? Are employees trained in the things that matter most? For example, if a hotel wants to maintain a welcoming atmosphere, are employees trained in welcoming? What is the total cost of training programs (including direct, indirect, and opportunity costs)? For example, if the company has a mentoring program, how much time does this require from mentors and protégés? What is the role of the mentor program in the overall training initiative? How do total costs break down by unit? By function? By program? What is the cost per employee? How do training costs compare to benchmark, best practices, and competitor costs? Are these costs growing? How fast? How do these costs stack up against the perceived *value* of the programs?

Bottom line: Plot the fit (high or low) and cost/value ratio (high or low) of training programs on a matrix.

Red flags for training: Low budget for training in comparison to benchmarks. No link to career development or succession planning.

Lack of training in basics. Trainee complaints that they have no say in programs—or that there are too many programs, too few, or not the right kind. Mentors complaining that the program takes too much time.

Assessment of Organizational Structure

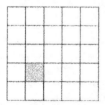

• *Outsourcing/insourcing.* Based on the findings of the initial clarification process, how does the current outsourcing/insourcing balance *fit* the company's strategy and culture with respect to senior managers, employees, and key stakeholders? For example, if there is a trend toward more outsourcing, what effect does this have on the morale of internal service providers? How do outsourced functions meet quality and customer service standards? How do outsourcing ratios compare to benchmark, best practices, and competitor costs? Is outsourcing particular functions more risky than keeping them in-house? If so, does management have a sense of the risk/reward ratio for outsourcing these high-risk functions? How can outsourcers be monitored? What is the *total cost* of outsourcing (including direct, indirect, and opportunity costs)? How do these costs break down by unit? By function? By program? What is the cost per employee? Are these costs growing? How fast? How do these costs stack up against the perceived *value* of the outsourcing? Has the company considered developing "shared services units" to serve the company and the marketplace on a profitmaking basis?

Bottom line: Plot the fit (high or low) and cost/value ratio (high or low) of career development programs on a matrix.

Red flags for outsourcing/insourcing: What is the company's current balance between internal and external providers of support services? Is this balance satisfactory for managers and other employees? Will the new strategy change this balance? In what areas? Who is monitoring the effectiveness of any outsourced functions?

- *HR function effectiveness.* Based on the findings of the initial clarification process, how does the company's current human resource function (which in some leading-edge companies is called the human capital function) *fit* the company's strategy and culture with respect to senior managers, employees, and key stakeholders? How responsive is the HR function to changes in business strategy? What is the ratio of HR staff to total staff? What is the *total cost* of the HR function (including direct, indirect, and opportunity costs)? For example, what is the salary of the HR director and what is his or her budget? What is the cost per employee based on these figures? How do HR program costs compare to benchmark, best practices, and competitor costs? Are these costs growing? How fast? How do these costs stack up against the perceived *value* of the function? Do HR managers see employees as their customers?

Bottom line: Plot the fit (high or low) and cost/value ratio (high or low) of the HR function on a matrix.

Red flags for HR function effectiveness: Perception of human resources "bureaucracy" based on paperwork and adding little value. Lack of channels for communication between the human resources director and senior management. Lack of "customer service" spirit in staff functions.

Assessment of HC Enablers

- *Legal and accounting compliance.* Based on the findings of the initial clarification process, how does the company's current compliance function *fit* the company's strategy and culture with respect to senior managers, employees, and key stakeholders? What is the balance of internal and external service providers in compliance? (See outsourcing/insourcing previously.) What is the *total cost* of the function (including direct, indirect, and opportunity costs)? For example, what is the salary of the compliance director and what is his or her budget? What is the cost per employee for all this? How do compliance program costs and legal fees compare to benchmark, best practices, and competitor costs? Are these costs growing? How fast? How do these costs stack up to the perceived value of the compliance programs?

  Bottom line: Plot the fit (high or low) and cost/value ratio (high or low) of compliance function on a matrix.

  Red flags for compliance: Heavy use of internal and external counsel to resolve conflicts. Size and frequency of lawsuits high in comparison to benchmark by industry and size of company.

- *Employee and industrial relations.* Based on the findings of the initial clarification process, how does the company's current employee and industrial relations program *fit* the company's strategy and culture with respect to senior managers, employees, and key stakeholders? What is the *total cost* of the function (including direct, indirect, and opportunity costs)? For example, is there an employee relations manager or ombudsman performing this function? What is his or her salary and budget? How does this cost and others stack up to perceived *value* of the program?

Bottom line: Plot the fit (high or low) and cost/value ratio (high or low) of the employee and industrial relations function on a matrix.

Red flags for employee and industrial relations: High turnover. Poor morale. Rumor mill is churning. Extended contract negotiations. High level of unresolved confrontation between employees.

- *Communications.* Based on the findings of the initial clarification process, how does the company's current communications function *fit* the company's strategy and culture with respect to senior managers, employees, and key stakeholders? Do employees value and trust the official communications they receive? What is the *total cost* of the communications function (including direct, indirect, and opportunity costs)? For example, does the company have a communications director? What percentage of the director's salary is spent on communicating with employees? How do costs stack up against the perceived *value* of the program?

  Bottom line: Plot the fit (high or low) and cost/value ratio (high or low) of the comunications function on a matrix.

  Red flags for communication: No mission statement or no employee awareness of existing mission statement. Excessive use of memos to conduct routine business. No comprehensive communications strategy for key initiatives.

- *Human resources information systems.* Based on the findings of the initial clarification process, how do the company's current human resources information systems *fit* the company's strategy and culture with respect to senior managers, employees, and key stakeholders? What is the *total cost* of the system (including direct, indirect, and opportunity costs)? For example, what is the average annual cost of upgrading? How do costs for the system compare to benchmark, best practices, and competitor costs? Are these costs growing? How fast? How do they stack up against the perceived *value* of the program?

Does the HR function produce timely, useful information that management can use in its reporting to internal and external groups?

Bottom line: Plot the fit (high or low) and cost/value ratio (high or low) of HRIS function on a matrix.

Red flags for human capital information systems: Complaints about information that is inaccurate or slow, about technology that is old or inappropriate, or about an information culture that is too "mechanical," or even "inhuman." Backlog of requests for training.

CONCLUSION

No firm wants leaders of human capital who "can't see the forest for the trees," as the old adage asserts. But neither do companies want leaders who "can't see the trees for the forest." The ability to appraise the "fit, cost, and value" of current human capital programs is a way of seeing both the big picture for human capital in a company and—equally important—all that it contains.

Chapter Six

DESIGN

Creating New Programs for Human Capital

Necessity is the mother of invention.

—Anonymous

In all the stages in human capital management, the *design* stage may well be the most challenging, because it beckons managers into a new realm of endeavor. Designers of human capital programs are called to be true artists as they move away from analysis and toward concerted action.

If managers have gone through the first two stages of the Human Capital Appraisal™ approach, they will be more than ready to meet this challenge. After seeing both the big picture and the details within it, they will have the broad and deep vision they need to go to work. Moreover, they will have clear goals for their task. Having plotted all current programs on a Fit-Cost-Value™ matrix, managers will have a good idea of which programs they need to replace (or simply cut), and which programs they need to maintain. Furthermore, they can see in what general way they need to improve these current programs—by reducing their costs, by aligning them with strategy, or by improving them in other ways unique to their situations.

DESIGNING HUMAN CAPITAL PROGRAMS: TWELVE "STEPS"

Companies will want to address not only the strategic fit and financial cost of a program; they will want to work on the new program's *human* fit and *human* cost. Will the program be accepted by the people it is targeting? If it is intended to serve or motivate, might it have any unanticipated negative side effects? These questions cannot be answered if the program design occurs in a vacuum. The designing cannot be done by an outside consultant. It must be done by company insiders—both in an oversight role (through a steering committee made up of senior managers), and in a design role (through a design team made up of stakeholders—managers and other employees affected by the new program—along with appropriate specialists). Consultants may advise either or both of these developments, but always from the side, never front and center.

The renewing process of design, like the human capital management process itself, occurs in stages—approximately twelve of them, in our experience. Because these are occurring within a larger stage, we will call them "steps." (See Box 6-1.)

This chapter is not organized by human capital areas, but rather by the twelve steps of design. The five areas of human capital will appear only peripherally as examples. (Also, as a constant reminder, they appear in Box 6-2.)

Once again, we remind readers that there is no magic in our numbers. We have found these processes to be convenient ways to group information, but readers are free to discover their own way of organizing experience. Although this process has met with repeated success in a variety of situations, we are not engraving these steps in stone quite yet. Far more important are the basic principles behind the steps: to have a rigorous, objective design process that suits the needs of the company, and to involve key stakeholders in that process.

Step 1: Company Forms Steering Committee

The first step in design is to form a *steering committee* that will have overall responsibility for the new program. This senior management

---

BOX 6-1
The Twelve Steps of Design

Step 1: Senior management selects steering committee
    Step 2: Steering committee assesses needs and readiness
    Step 3: Steering committee determines objectives
    Step 4: Steering committee selects participants in plan
Step 5: Steering committee selects design team
    Step 6: Design team confirms focus
    Step 7: Design team assesses current state
    Step 8: Design team envisions future state
    Step 9: Design team designs new program
      Determination of performance measurements
      Definition of terms
      Definition of duration
      Structure of program
    Step 10: Design team prepares report
    Step 11: Design team presents report
Step 12: Steering committee amends/approves design team report

---

team should be largely self-selected, evolving naturally from the needs of the company. It will include the senior officers who are concerned about the problem that the new program is designed to solve. The steering committee's task is to formulate guidelines for a program based on the findings of the Fit-Cost-Value™ sessions. The steering committee is the initiating sponsor of the program.

Step 2: Steering Committee Assesses Needs and Readiness

This step begins with two fundamental questions: Why a new plan? Is the company ready? (See Box 6-2.) As for the need, there may not be one. If the current plan has a low cost and a high fit/value ratio, why argue with success?

Remember, all change has a cost. Introducing change for the sake of change is never wise. All too often, managers will say to us: "Sales are down, profits are down. We need to increase our performance. So design a pay-for-performance plan for us." We always ask them to step back and

---

BOX 6-2
Check Your Motives

QUESTION: DO WE (REALLY) NEED A NEW PLAN FOR:

Recruitment, retention, and retirement (e.g., diversity, critical skills)?

Performance management and rewards?

Career development, succession planning, and training?

Organizational design (e.g., outsourcing/insourcing, HC effectiveness)?

HC enablers (e.g., compliance, employee relations, communication, information, technology)?

ANSWER: IT DEPENDS ON WHAT WE LEARNED IN THE ASSESSMENT STAGE!

---

see where the problem and the need for change really are. (See Box 6-2.) Is it really the compensation system—or are there other areas that need work, perhaps involving the culture itself?

Even when there is a need, it is important to ask if the organization is ready to meet it. One of the roles of the steering committee will be to oversee the change management process. At this stage, the committee reviews the organization's readiness for change and its track record in managing change—laying the groundwork for action later on.

To give direction to their work, some steering committees find it useful to use a facilitator—a neutral person, often a consultant from outside the organization, who helps the group structure a process for working and making decisions together. The facilitator may be skilled in the branch of consulting called "participative process consulting." True to his or her name, the facilitator is there to make thing easy—not to make particular things happen or even to advise on content. The facilitator should not have any personal interest in the program being designed (and therefore no conflicts of interest). To ensure objectivity, the facilitator can be hired and compensated by the board of directors, rather than by management.

Step 3: Steering Committee Determines Objectives.

In the first two stages of human capital management, we saw that thoroughness was the key: *Every* area of human capital merits clarification and assessment. Design is another matter. In this highly creative realm, *selectivity* is the password to success. Given enough money and freedom, managers may be tempted to replace or fix programs that already work, or to build new programs where one—or even none—will do. They must resist this impulse and replace it with a single mission: to respond to need. For it is not whim but necessity, driven by the findings of the clarification and assessment stages, that will generate true inventions in the workplace. (As the old Latin saying goes, *Mater artium necessitas*—Necessity is the mother of invention.) Managers must focus their energies and efforts, exploring design options *only* in areas of concern. No matter how enticing a fresh start in other areas may seem along the way, managers must tackle first things first. The aim of this process is not to reengineer but to renovate.

Setting *objectives* can help. In this step, the primary question is simple: What are you hoping to achieve with the new plan?

Possible goals for *recruitment* and *retention* plans, as well as for the timing aspects of *retirement* policies, include:

- Increase diversity (better balance of age, gender, race).
- Increase market share (by hiring representatives in a particular region).
- Reduce employee turnover (through "golden handcuffs" and non-competes).

New plans in the *performance management and rewards* area might aim to:

- Increase revenues (by tying pay/promotions to revenue increases).
- Increase profits (by tying pay to profit increases).
- Reduce absenteeism (by rewarding attendance/penalizing absence).
- Motivate group teamwork (through group gain-sharing).

- Motivate individual performance (through specific performance targets).

Goals for new *career development, succession planning,* and *training* programs might be to:

- Increase productivity (through increasing motivation and skills).
- Increase knowledge base of company (by results-oriented development/training).
- Increase employee awareness of corporate goals (by training staff in goals).
- Enhance value of intellectual property (as a direct result of the previous actions).
- Ensure appropriate succession into key roles (including the CEO role).

Changes in *organization design* (including insourcing/outsourcing and the overall human capital function), might be needed to:

- Reduce number of purely administrative positions (and conversely building line jobs).
- Increase organizational/financial efficiency (by eliminating redundancy and waste).
- Increase capital investment (attracting shareholders and/or lenders as a result of increased efficiency).

Systems-oriented managers will notice at once that many of the goals that appear under one area might also be satisfied by initiatives in other areas. For example, the goal of increasing market share might be satisfied not only through recruitment, but also through rewards.

Also, some goals may be in conflict. For example, in any plan, an emphasis on revenue growth and/or market share may necessitate a temporary downturn in profits. Conversely, an emphasis on profits may mean a period of low growth. Also, incentives for teams may demotivate individual effort, while incentives for individuals may disrupt teams. There are ways to satisfy both goals—usually through multiple or complex plans.

Finally, managers may want to make changes in systems that work as human capital *enablers,* such as compliance systems. Unlike the other areas of human capital management, which are ends unto themselves, enablers are means to an end. Therefore, improvement efforts are usually devoted to strengthening the program itself (or a particular aspect of it), rather than an area outside the program. For example, managers might strive to:

- Strengthen accounting/legal compliance (especially environmental compliance).
- Build better employee relations (especially between union members and management).
- Improve communications (especially upstream—staff-to-management).
- Redesign information systems (especially client-server technology).

Step 4: Steering Committee Selects the Plan Targets

Managers who know *why* they want a new plan are well on their way to the next step—identifying participants. This is not surprising, for although human capital management may be a process, the validity and reality of this process begins and ends with people. So very early on in the design process it will be time to ask *who*—who will be a participant in the new program?

As a general rule, there is no point in involving employees whose contribution to the corporate objective is likely to be minimal or nonexistent. For example, if the goal of an incentive plan is to increase revenues and market shares, it makes more sense to include the sales force than it does to include the internal auditing staff. By contrast, a profit-based plan for a fast-growing company with internal control problems should definitely involve the internal auditing staff.

This is not to say that incentive schemes are only right for those who influence performance directly, such as senior managers and salespeople. It all depends on the objective. For example, if the goal of a new incentive pay plan is to increase the performance of a particular team, then obviously all team members should participate in it. By contrast, if the objective of the pay plan is to increase individual performance, then the plan can be more discriminating, including only individuals whose unique contributions can be measured. If a company is trying to achieve multiple objectives with a pay plan, it may need more than one plan to achieve them.

The example we just cited features pay plans, but this is not the only type of human capital program that has participants. Consider:

- In *recruitment, retention, and retirement,* **who** besides designated recruiters can help attract talent to the organization? Who besides the human resources director can become a part of retention and retirement planning?
- In *performance management* as well as *rewards,* **whose** performance needs a boost? Even if one group is the main focus, should another group be included because of its working ties to the focus group?
- In *career development, succession planning, and training,* **who** should be on the line-manager development track? What groups need training in what subjects?
- In *organizational design,* **whose** jobs will change? For example, **whose** jobs may be eliminated or converted to contract labor due to outsourcing, or, conversely, **who** among suppliers could lose their contracts because of a move toward insourcing? **Who** besides the human resources staff will be involved in increasing HR effectiveness?

Step 5: Steering Committee Selects Design Team

Once the steering committee has assessed needs and readiness, determined goals, and identified participants, its active work is over. From now on it will simply monitor, handing the torch of initiative over to the internal *design team.* The job of this team is to attend a *set amount of meetings* structured with *predetermined goals*—goals that take the group through the design process in a limited amount of time, typically six months, with one meeting per month. (See Box 6-3.) Design team members are sustaining sponsors and change agents.

BOX 6-3
Design Team Meetings: The Key to Success

The design team members must make a commitment to attend all meetings of the design team. Our experience shows that the following meetings *at a minimum* are critical to team success:

Design Meeting # 1: Confirming the focus

Design Meeting #2: Assessing the current state

Design Meeting #3: Envisioning the future state

Design Meeting #4: Designing the new program

Design Meeting # 5: Preparing the report and cost analysis

Design Meeting # 6: Presenting the report to the steering committee.

As mentioned, in appointing and empowering design team members, the steering committee should include at least one representative of the employees who will be most closely affected by the new program being designed. The following examples illustrate this stakeholder principle. They are not ironclad rules, but they show ways to involve stakeholders. Common sense will dictate your choice.

If your team is designing a new:

- *salesforce recruitment program* designed to expand into a new geographic territory, include at least one sales manager of an existing territory.
- *recruitment program* targeting a specific group (new college graduates, senior-level women, minority engineers), include at least one current employee from the target group.
- *retention program* targeting a specific area, include at least one former employee from that area whose stated reasons for resignation were company-related (not entirely personal).
- *retirement policy and pay program,* include a range of employees by age, and at least one employee nearing retirement under the current system.

- *performance management program for plant supervisors,* include at least one plant supervisor—and someone who reports directly to a plant supervisor (from two different plants).
- *succession plan for the CEO position,* include the CEO.
- *training program for engineers,* include at least one engineer.
- labor law compliance program, include the current compliance officer and one direct report.

In addition to stakeholders, the design team should include someone from the human resources function who has a broad overview of the company's existing programs. And the committee should include appropriate internal *technical specialists*—from accounting, finance, law, information systems, or whatever is needed. For example, a new retirement plan should certainly include an expert in pension law. If the company lacks the expertise needed, it can include an external expert as an ad-hoc member to the committee. This member should advise the committee, but should have no voting power.

In selecting stakeholders, human resources staffers, and technical specialists for the design team, the steering committee should look for two important qualities:

- First, an ability to work with a team. This is not the place to include the brilliant contrarian or the would-be whistle-blower. These countercultural personalities have great value to the organization in general, and may be invited to make presentations to the design team, but they are not conducive to achieving consensus—an important function of the design team.
- Second, a commitment to attend all meetings of the team. As described in Box 6-3, our experience shows that meetings are critical to the success of a design team, and that the group will need at least six meetings to achieve its work.

Finally, in selecting members of the design team, the steering committee should include members from other design teams from related programs, so that there are interlocks among all design teams. For example, suppose a company wants to start a new program to recruit minority sales managers and at the same time to restructure the pay of all sales managers around a new performance goal. This typically would require two design teams, a recruitment team and a pay team. Someone from the recruitment team should also sit in as an "ambassador" on the pay team. Because this may require attendance at a dozen meetings, often the best choice is one of the HR staffers who sits on one of the teams, rather than one of the stakeholders or technical specialists. (Indeed, the design process highlights the importance and usefulness of having dedicated HR professionals on staff, and shows how such professionals can link their work to strategy.)

As mentioned in Figure 6-3, design team members should sign a contract pledging attendance at all meetings of the design team. As a practical matter, this means in effect that employees unwilling to sign a "contract"—written or verbal—should not be invited onto the team. Meetings carry through the next six steps in the design process.

Step 6: Design Team Confirms Focus and Plans Communication

The first meeting of the design team is absolutely critical—with benefits that extend far beyond the immediate occasion. At this important gathering, the team reviews the steering committee's parameters and guidelines. Team members will be grounded in the fundamentals of change management, as well as in key results of the steering committee's work. Often itself an assessment of change management potential, this first meeting becomes a barometer of the degree of connection between those at the executive level and those further on down the line.

The first meeting establishes working relationships among team members. They start the process of "contracting" with each other: ground rules are established and specific roles are assigned.

At this first meeting another important goal should be accomplished: the establishment of a subcommittee to form communications strategy. A subteam should be formed to determine how the work of the committee will be communicated on a regular and timely basis. Communication formats might include "town meetings," videos, and publishing the minutes of design team meetings. Regular communication will not only increase the chances that employees will "buy in" to the plan; it will also provoke commentary that can be taken into consideration as the design process continues. At the end of its work, this committee will be charged with communication of the final plan (see Step 12). As mentioned earlier, a facilitator can help in this process.

Step 7: Design Team Assesses Current State

At their second meeting, team members assess two key forces underlying the design process: corporate readiness for change, and the current functionality of the program being changed. The exercise is diagnostic. The team is asked to consider questions such as the following:

- What kind of corporate culture are we in? (This is drawing from the clarification stage findings.)
- What is its propensity for change?
- How do people in the company respond to change?
- How have change initiatives been greeted in the past?
- Have those changes been successful? If not, why not?

In answering these questions, the team members will look closely at the current state of the program to be redesigned, and how the program links with other programs in the company.

Step 8: Design Team Extends Vision of Future State

In their next meeting, the design team faces in the direction set by the steering committee, but extends its vision farther still, based on findings and insights generated by the current-state assessment. Team members may identify new roles and behaviors required to accomplish desired steering committee goals. They look at where the company is now and where it would like to be, and what will be required to close identified gaps. They explore which performance measures will generate which outcomes, creating valuable concepts to be nailed down at their next meeting. Building on their collective vision of the future, they discuss how to prepare for these changes, how to close existing gaps, and how much time is required to achieve the future state.

To facilitate brainstorming, future-state design might also include best-practice discussions, reviewing earlier answers to the questions asked in the clarification and assessment stages—namely "What fits our company best?" and "What is working and what is not working?" It might include benchmarking other companies of similar size and product/service range. (For more on benchmarking, see Chapter 9.)

Step 9: Design Team Designs the New Program

All of the above steps have really been preparation for the one that matters most—the actual creation of the new program. By the time managers reach this step, they should be well prepared for it. They will have established a true need for the program, satisfying themselves that this is not change merely for the sake of change. They will know exactly *why* they are designing the program, *who* will be a participant involved in the program, and *how* the success of the program and its participants will be measured. Now it is time for the *what:* the program itself.

Every program is unique, and one type of program will be very different from another type. For example, the process of creating a new retirement policy may have little or nothing in common with the process of creating a new program for human capital information systems. Nonetheless, some fundamentals do apply.

The following checklist sets out some of the most important features or "design dimensions" to consider in designing any new human capital program or plan.

Design Dimensions to Consider

• *Determining the performance measurement(s) to be used in the plan.* Most plans in the human capital arena have some performance dimension. The notion of "pay for performance" is virtually ingrained in management thinking around the world today. From ventures sketched on the back of an envelope to far-flung multinational empires, the notion of rewarding effort is universal. But what about performance measurements in the other areas of human capital? This idea is less common but no less important. How should a plan define performance? The basic answer is simple: Performance means achievement of stated goals. If your goal for a particular program is to increase market share, then you should *measure performance based on achievement of that goal.*

The challenge, of course, is in the details: How much market share, where, in what demographic group, at what rate over what period? Managers need to identify as many expectations as they can for inclusion in the plan. Moreover, managers need to ascertain whether these goals (and related performance measurements) are reasonable. Is it fair to expect a doubling of market share in a year? In most cases, no. Goals and performance targets should be set with care; they must motivate, not dispirit.

- *Definition of key terms used in the plan.* Long before the plan must be implemented and communicated, its key words must be determined and defined. In particular, plan creators should clearly define words or phrases that have a specific meaning in the context of the company or that are open to misinterpretation.
- *Duration of the plan.* Is it for a specific calendar period, will it last until a specific goal has been met, or will it be in force as long as it is useful? In the last case, is there a sunset clause to ensure ongoing usefulness (e.g., annual review and renewal)? In any event, either the termination date or period should be determined in advance, or some statement should be made as to the mechanism for terminating the plan. For example, the plan might stipulate that it will be in effect "until the Company's Board of Directors votes for termination of the plan, to be reviewed annually by the Board Management Committee."
- *Structure of the plan.* This is the nitty-gritty part, where technical specialists are most likely to be involved. Each area will have its own structural considerations. For example, in designing a pension plan, this would be the time to discuss plan liability with an actuary, and to draft plan type (defined benefit versus defined contribution, qualified versus nonqualified, funded versus unfunded). Organizations should search for best practices in the pension practices of their peers. They should also consider the impact of recent legislation (almost an annual event in many countries). In designing an incentive plan, con-

siderations will include: calculating the incentive payment, distribution of the incentive payment; floors and ceilings; timing of the payment, ending of employment; change of control conditions.

Here, too, having an expert to advise on current regulations will be helpful.

At this design meeting, consultants with the relevant content expertise may present design concepts, how each works, their trade-offs, and so forth. The presentation is highly interactive, with participants discussing and reviewing a variety of design alternatives with the team. At the conclusion of this meeting, the consultants and the team will have a clear idea of the general plan construct and the performance measures that are to be reinforced with the new program. The team will also have validated the design against the parameters established for the design—and will be ready to work on modeling details.

Step 10: Design Team Prepares Report and Cost Analysis

This is a nuts-and-bolts meeting. Someone will model the new program based on the company's or unit's financial and operating results for the previous year, then look at how the same program would apply to expected results for the current year. If program results cannot be expected to yield reasonable return on investment, a redesign effort will likely take place. The goal for this meeting is to design a program that makes business sense for the company, as well as having the best possible fit with the company's strategy.

Step 11: Design Team Presents Report to the Steering Committee

Now the design team presents the results to the steering committee. Team members explain why the design makes good business sense, backed up by the consultants who helped devise the new program. The presentation must assure the steering committee that the redesigned program supports the company's business objectives, enhances individual performance, and results in a positive return on investment. If the business case justifies it, the design committee may even ask the steering committee to modify its original guidelines and design parameters.

Step 12: Steering Committee Amends/Approves/Communicates Design Team Report

Then, based on agreed modifications and the convergence of the steering committee and design team thinking, the new plan is approved and communicated. During the communication process, all stakeholders in the plan should be informed about it, including not only employees but also investors and other concerned parties. The plan is now ready for the next step: *implementation* (covered in the next chapter).

CONCLUSION

Poet T. S. Eliot captured an important truth when he wrote that

> *Between the idea*
> *And the reality . . .*
> *Falls the Shadow*

Design, the stage that falls between the idea of a program and its actual implementation, can seem very much like a shadow—a black box where creative experts do their work apart from the operational mainstream. But the design phase offers more than this. Design can and must be a dynamic process in which flesh-and-blood managers respond to the only true mother of invention in human capital programs: strategic necessity.

Chapter Seven

IMPLEMENTATION

Making Human Capital Programs Work

Order is not pressure that is imposed from without, but an
equilibrium that is set up from within.

—Ortega y Gasset, *Mirabeau and Politics*

After a company envisions a direction for its human capital programs, takes an accurate measure of its present course, and de-
signs the ways its people must progress from the present to the future,
its work may seem almost over—and yet in one way, it is just beginning.
For after the stages of clarification, assessment, and design comes a
phase that can make all the difference between success and failure—*implementation.*

Now comes a quantum leap—turning paper goals into real-time results. This means "making it happen" in some areas and "letting it happen" in others, as managers become not only forces for change, but
empowerers of change. But how?

In our experience working with hundreds of clients, there is a close
equivalence between the effort expended at the beginning stages of a
change process—the "alpha" of strategic clarification and assessment—
and the ease possible during the last stages—the "omega" of implementation and monitoring. The middle stage, design, seeks to bridge the
two, functioning very much like an equal sign.

Alpha truly is omega here: Every good decision made in the very beginning erases a potential problem down the road in the end, and every poor decision creates one. In this broad sense, if managers have done all the necessary preparatory work, implementation can be almost a matter of simple mechanics—merely a matter of assigning responsibilities and setting timetables. But as any manager involved with new human capital programs knows, programs that involve real people with real jobs (as opposed to organizational charts in a computer) can never be mechanized. "Popular mechanics" is a great name for a magazine, but not for the workplace, where mechanistic schemes are bound to fail. So how can managers maintain acceptance (if not popularity) for the rollout of a new program?

This is an urgent question, because the majority of change initiatives fail during the implementation stage, according to research by David Nadler, a consultant in organizational change who has edited and authored numerous books in the areas. Nadler, a former faculty member at the Graduate School of Business at Columbia University and a staff member at the Institute for Social Research at the University of Michigan, is well-known for his axes of quality and implementation, which show a minor role for the former and a major role for the latter: Most change initiatives (80 percent) fail because of poor implementation, Nadler has found. (See Box 7-1.)

"SIX PLUS" TOOLS FOR IMPLEMENTATION

In the previous chapter, we outlined twelve suggested steps in the design process. In doing so, we advised managers to create their own processes, using our experience as a mere starting point. In the same spirit, we now suggest several tools for implementation, intended for adaptation to a company's own circumstances. Flexibility must rule,

---

BOX 7-1
The Axes of Quality and Implementation

Bad Idea, Good Implementation 10%	Good Idea, Good Implementation 10%
Bad Idea, Bad Implementation 10%	**Good Idea, Bad Implementation 70%**

now that we are out of the blueprint room and into the hurly-burly of operating reality. These tools really are more like checklist points; they *need not be used sequentially—and some are ongoing*. For example, the process of communicating a new program (discussed at the end of this section) begins before the implementation stage begins and continues long after it ends.

Tool 1: The Point Person

Most new programs—whether in recruitment, in rewards, or any other area—can benefit from having a formal or informal "point person"— someone who knows about the program and who is responsible for its implementation. The choice of this person will depend on the program, but typically it is an operating manager advised by the stakeholder member of the design committee who functioned as an ambassador during the creation of the new program. This person can be considered the key sustaining sponsor.

Tool 2: The Pilot Program

As the first stage in launching a new program, consider "piloting" it. There are various ways to pilot a new program. The company can launch the entire program, but only with a certain group of employees—for example, managers (this will counter any impression employees may have that the program is being foisted on them from above). Another way to pilot a program is to run it on a voluntary basis before making it mandatory. Finally, instead of running the full program for only a small number of people (managers or volunteers in these examples), the program could be run only in part, with other parts of the program to roll out later. Whichever piloting method is chosen, the pilot is a good way of working out problems before they happen. Once any issues have been resolved, the program may be extended from the pilot.

Tool 3: Training Links

Managers and administrators may need to be trained in the new program—why it was established and how it works. The training program may use the company's existing infrastructure for training, or it may require extra help from the outside. For example, in introducing a new performance management system, the company might have a workshop to refresh employees' knowledge of "who, what, where, when, and why"—who will be the point person on the program and who the program will affect, what the program will entail, where the program will begin (in the case of a pilot) and where it will expand, and, most important, more and varied reminders of why the program began.

Tool 4: Policy and Process Links

Any new program is bound to have interconnections with existing processes in the company. Although some of these relationships may be built into the design, others may be left to chance. The managers implementing the new program would be wise to anticipate some of the interfaces. One way to do this is to identify the key processes of the company, and to use them as a checklist for implementation planning. As an aid to this process, managers might use Arthur Andersen's list of all the processes and subprocesses a company may have. It can be found on our Web site www.arthurandersen.com/best practices.

Tool 5: Feedback

Feedback is good anytime, anywhere, but it is particularly important during a time of transition for a human capital program. Managers should encourage employees to channel their feedback on a new program into ideas for action: What should we do more of? What should we stop doing? What should we do differently? What should we start doing?

Tool 6: Documentation

Managers should consider maintaining a written record of the rollout of the new program. Part of this written record will already exist as an outgrowth of the design process. For example, if the company is implementing a "360 degree" program for employee evaluation (getting evaluated by peers and subordinates as well as by supervisors), it will no doubt already have a program description in writing. But managers

should also make ongoing documentation of how the program is used—
a point to be covered in more detail in the next chapter, "Monitoring."

Tool "Infinity": Communication

Implementing any new human capital program requires first and foremost communications through the regular channels. In most companies,
these include:

- Briefings (for teams).
- Executive visits/exchanges.
- Management information (memos, notices, operational instructions,
  telephone and address lists).
- Management road shows.
- One-on-one meetings (between managers and subordinates, or be-
  tween peers).
- Publications (employee newsletters).
- Staff meetings (for some or all staff).
- Working groups (task forces, project teams).

Through these varied means, managers and others can communicate
the technical content and motivational meaning of the new program to
all affected employees. The balance of content and meaning in these
communications will depend very much on the situation at hand (see
Box 7-2).

Of course, the quality of communications about the new program will
depend in part on the way the company already communicates. In larger
companies, there is often a formal function called "employee communications." Sometimes, this function is one of the human capital areas
being changed, and managers are charged with ensuring good communications *about* communications—not an easy task. The temptation here
will be to ask employees to "do what I say, not what I do," yet it is what
managers do that will communicate the most clearly. Here more than in
any area, managers must lead by example.

Whether managers are ensuring good communications about a new
communications program or about a new pension plan, there are some

---

BOX 7-2
Communicating a New Compliance Program:
Contrasting Examples

Consultants often advise managers to "communicate" a new program to all employees. But different situations require different modes and styles of communication. Consider an example from the area of labor law compliance—say, a new program designed to increase compliance with equal opportunity regulations, especially with respect to gender issues. Two different companies might design programs for different reasons, and implement them in different ways, using two very different types of communication style.

Both companies might design initiatives to increase male-female balance in the workplace with respect to recruitment, promotions, teamwork, and relations between employees (including issues of sexual harassment)—all with the goal of a better compliance profile. Depending on the reason for the program, though, the emphasis of the communication efforts might be different. Here are two "composite cases" based on real situations.

- *Situation:* This company and the great majority of its employees believe that it has a relatively good working climate for women—not a "hostile environment," to use legal language. The impetus for the compliance program was a lawsuit filed by an individual employee naming an individual manager whose behavior was in a gray area. The company has never been accused of this problem before, either externally or internally (through its complaint process). It is starting the program because it is concerned that managers may make innocent mistakes that could lead to future legal troubles.
- *Style:* For this company, the emphasis should be on low-cost, efficient information: Managers should receive information detailing exactly what behavior is against the law. The centerpiece of communication efforts could be a written handbook. The likely result? A workforce that knows more about the law, and is protected from frivolous litigation.

- *Situation:* In this case, the company believes that it has a poor working climate for women—the classic "hostile environment." The impetus for the new program was a class action filed by a large group of female employees following numerous internal complaints.
- *Style:* In this situation, informing employees of their legal obligations and rights will do some good, but managers will need to concentrate first on getting the employees to care about, trust in, and understand the law in the first place. Although management may distribute a handbook, this will support a broader agenda of face-to-face communications on the connection between compliance and company values. Ideal result for this company: Eradication of any gender bias.

These sample cases are about gender relations, but they could be about any potential area of liability. Depending on the extent and nature of the problem, solutions will differ.

best practices to follow. Communication efforts will cover a multitude of smaller steps—each unique to the program at hand.

CONCLUSION

Most human capital initiatives fail not because of failures in planning, assessment, or design. The point of failure comes during the implementation phase. This phase is unique to the program being implemented and the organization doing the implementation, yet some general principles apply—what we call the tools of implementation. Beyond this, companies must travel their own roads to implementation.

Chapter Eight

MONITORING

Tracking Human Capital Initiatives Against Strategy

It takes a long time to bring excellence to maturity.

—Publilius Syrus, *Maxims*

Monitoring should be the final and definitive stage in the management of any new human capital program. All too often, however, it is the forgotten stage—a vague resolution fading into the background as newer, brighter endeavors burst on the scene.

In too many companies, programs appear like fireworks—each one louder and bigger than the last, but all eventually fading into embers and ashes. A case in point is the anonymous company featured in the beginning of *Human Resource Champions* (1997), by Dave Ulrich, a professor in the School of Business at the University of Michigan and a fellow in the National Academy of Human Resources. This company, says Ulrich, tried *twenty-two initiatives in just ten years*—more than two per year! Here is the mind-numbing list:

- Business-process reengineering
- Business unit restructuring
- Continuous improvement
- Consolidation
- Corporate-centers study

- Cost analysis
- Cycle time
- Decentralization
- Downsizing
- Economic value-added

- Empowerment
- Excellence
- Goal-setting
- Japanese management (Theory Z)
- Leadership development
- Mission, vision, and values

- Quality
- Restructuring
- Rewards and recognition
- Six Sigma
- Variable pay
- Workout

One can only imagine how jaded the employees of this change-addicted company must have been when the eighth (or eighteenth) new initiative rolled around. The French have a saying for this: *Tout nouveau, tout beau.* Freely translated (giving words to the ironic tone of voice) this means, "Fools see beauty only in new things." How true this is—yet how prone we all can be to such folly. It is more fun to reinvent a wheel than to repair an old one. Fun, yes; wise, no!

So let us consider the wise alternative. Suppose this same company had initiated just one or two of these programs and then followed through with them, monitoring them carefully over time to see just what adjustments they might need, and applying continuous improvement. This approach may well have reduced the number of initiatives sweeping through this company, producing the same or better results with less trauma to the organization.

The term *monitoring* has various meanings—from the general notion of keeping watch over something, to the very specific act of testing for radiation intensity. In our view, the latter definition is closer to the truth! Monitoring cannot be a mere attitude—it must be a series of actions. To monitor the success of a new human capital program, managers must *measure it against the original goals it was meant to accomplish.* Without this important finale, no human capital program can grow to its full potential.

MONITORING: AN IMPORTANT STAGE

In throwing down this gauntlet, we reveal our bias as partners in one of the world's largest and oldest accounting and consulting firms—a firm deeply involved in the setting of accounting and reporting standards both nationally and globally. More than any other professionals, accountants understand the importance of monitoring. For managers, this function is important, but for accountants it virtually epitomizes their calling.

One authoritative source on the subject of monitoring is the group called COSO, the Committee of Sponsoring Organizations, a group of accountants and others set up in the United States over a decade ago to prevent fraud. (For a detailed explanation of COSO, see Sources for Chapter 8.) COSO's major work, published in 1992 and updated in 1994, is *Internal Control: Integrated Framework*. In this report, COSO offers a very good checklist of the kind of work that monitoring can accomplish. The COSO discussion refers specifically to monitoring an internal control system, but COSO's findings are also applicable to the monitoring of human capital programs. The following discussion is modeled closely on this landmark document.

THE KEY POINTS OF MONITORING

Ongoing monitoring occurs in the ordinary course of operations, and includes regular management and supervisory activities that assess how well a system is performing. Monitoring is an important phase for any system, including a new human capital program such as a new pay plan, a new work-share program, or a new information system.

The quality of monitoring following the introduction of a new human capital program can be judged by many factors, including:

- The extent to which personnel, in carrying out their regular activities, obtain evidence as to whether the new program continues to function.
- The extent to which communications from external parties about the new program corroborate internally generated information, or indicate problems.
- Periodic assessment of the achievements of the new program in comparison to the goals set for it.
- Responsiveness to internal and external suggestions on means to strengthen the new program.

- The extent to which training seminars, planning sessions, and other meetings provide feedback to management on whether the new program is operating effectively.
- The effectiveness of support for the program—in particular, appropriate levels of competent and experienced staff and advisers to administer and advise the program, as needed.

THE ROLE OF PERIODIC FORMAL EVALUATION

In addition to ongoing monitoring activities, it may be appropriate to have periodic formal evaluations of a program to make sure that it is still functioning well—and indeed is still needed! A program may already have a sunset clause forcing closure in the absence of a vote for extension—but this is (unfortunately) extremely rare. As mentioned earlier in Chapter 6, systems all too often perpetuate themselves indefinitely, leading to low management productivity.

Harvard's Robert Simons and Antonio Davila, writing in the January–February 1998 issue of the *Harvard Business Review*, ask a pertinent question: "How High is Your Return on Management?" Simons and Davila note that management productivity suffers when "systems have a life of their own." Simons and Davila focus only on planning, budgeting, and control systems, but these are not the only systems that can assume perpetual life.

The danger of perpetuity is present in any system—indeed, especially in human capital programs, given their frequent popularity. We all know the national hue and cry that greets attempts to cut existing social programs, even when the need for the programs has waned, while the need for other, more worthy, causes goes unsatisfied. The same protests can occur when management reconsiders existing human capital programs to make room for new ones.

Obviously, the review of a popular human capital system must be done with sensitivity, and an effort to preserve all that is good. The point is, though, that it must be done. In the words of Arthur Miller, writing about Willy Loman in *Death of a Salesman*, "Attention must be paid!" (Loman, we remember, got overtaken as an individual salesman by the relentless collectivity of so-called business progress. In this same spirit, when looking at a system, we have to look for its invisible victims—sometimes politically incorrect causes like sales!) And this attention must be paid both in the ongoing monitoring system and in occasional formal review. The review should ask whether the program under review is serving the company's strategic purposes, and whether it is functioning effectively.

Qualities necessary for this periodic formal review include:

- *Scope and frequency.* Is the evaluation done deeply, broadly, and often enough? These will depend, in part, on the nature of the program and the stakes involved. A senior-executive stock option program's effectiveness might be evaluated annually, whereas the effectiveness of a new communications program aimed at increasing plant safety should be evaluated monthly or even weekly. A mitigating factor here is the strength of ongoing monitoring systems that are already built into the program.
- *Measurement.* Is the evaluation being done with the right focus? Does the evaluator understand the purpose of the program, how it works, and what results it is supposed to deliver? Does it have clear benchmarks or goals to measure against? For example, let us assume that a job-sharing plan was introduced primarily to increase morale and secondarily to increase productivity. The evaluation system should have a way to assess both factors, and to give them their relative importance.
- *Objectivity.* Are the right people doing the evaluation—people with the appropriate knowledge, skills, and authority, and the appropriate degree of independence? Program stakeholders may be qualified to evaluate a program, and may have valuable input into evaluation, but they should not be in charge—precisely because they have a vested interest in the program.
- *Appropriateness.* Is the evaluation being done in the right way? Are there appropriate checklists and questionnaires or other tools? If more than one evaluator is involved, have they coordinated their efforts? Does the person in charge have the appropriate level of authority to make changes in the program?

Any problems or shortfalls that are revealed during ongoing monitoring or periodic formal evaluation should be reported to the appropriate parties. There should be a regular mechanism for such reports. Deficiencies should be reported to the person directly responsible for the program and to the person one level up. When a problem is reported, there should be an effort to find out its root cause, and to correct it as soon as possible.

MONITORING FOR STRATEGIC FIT

One of the most important aspects of monitoring—yet the one that is most often overlooked—is monitoring for *strategic fit*. The strategic purpose for a new program will have been set during the clarification stage. Now is the time to return to that stage, asking: Is the new program working?

Some very helpful guidance in this regard comes from Christopher Mabey and Paul Iles, in their article "The Strategic Integration of Assessment and Development Practices: Succession Planning and New Manager Development" in *Human Resource Management Journal*, as noted earlier in Chapter 4. Mabey and Iles say that strategic integration needs to be understood in terms of at least three conceptually distinct (but often empirically related) dimensions.

- The first is *external integration*, which refers to HR's link to corporate strategy. This may be administrative (purely operational links), one way (HR programs react to strategy), two way (with reciprocal, interdependent links between HR and strategy), and integrating (with frequent, dynamic interaction between equal partners).
- The second is *institutional integration*, which has to do with the integration between HR and the personnel function.
- The third is *internal integration*, which refers to the coherent, consistent, interconnected application of a set of HR policy "levers."

In our view, the first type of integration is the most crucial—that is, the link of human capital programs to corporate strategy.

As consultants, we often recommend that a company perform an abbreviated Fit-Cost-Value™ analysis on the results of its new plans twelve to eighteen months after they are implemented. At the very least, new programs must be reviewed in light of new strategies that may have emerged over time.

CONCLUSION

Often overlooked, the monitoring stage of human capital management requires attention and diligence. Although it is the fifth and "final" stage of any management process, monitoring is never done. It must be ongoing. Standard procedures for monitoring, as taught by accounting professionals, can be very useful in checking for the continued usefulness of any program.

In closing, we would like to sound a positive note. Monitoring is not just about finding faultlines. It can also be about finding gold—real results from more focused investments in human capital. When the numbers show improvements, then a business case for human capital can be made—thus advancing the cause of human capital within an organization. Human resources managers, no longer seen in a merely administrative light, become true members of senior management—and sometimes even local heroes. In turn, senior managers seek alliances with HR in order to get more involved in the strategic management of human capital—the subject of our next chapter.

Chapter Nine

ASSESSING HUMAN CAPITAL FIT

Strategies for All Seasons

It was *déjà vu* all over again.

—Yogi Berra (attributed)

How can organizations determine the fit between their human capital programs and their strategy? If you experience "déjà vu all over again" in contemplating this question, you have understood our main message. Readers who have journeyed to this point now have heard about the importance of fit five times over: We said fit—along with cost and value—must be discovered in the clarification stage, measured in the assessment stage, forged in the design stage, supported in the implementation stage, and checked in the monitoring stage.

In the following three chapters, we will go more fully into questions of fit, cost, and value, exploring their deeper implications. In this chapter, we will not merely preach through theory (in the first part of the chapter) but also practice through example—showing exactly *how* fit may be assessed. Managers who wish to go straight to the practice part can skip to the next section, which explains how to apply the theory by assessing fit in an actual company.

FIT IN THEORY

How exactly can a human resources area, for example compensation, fit a strategy? On the theory front, some very helpful concepts come from Christopher Mabey and Paul Iles, in "The Strategic Integration of Assessment and Development Practices: Succession Planning and New Manager Development" in *Human Resource Management Journal,* as noted in earlier chapters.

To recap the previous chapter, Mabey and Iles say that strategic integration needs to be understood in terms of at least three dimensions. The first is *external integration,* which refers to HR's links to corporate strategy. The second is *institutional integration,* which has to do with the integration between HR and the personnel function. The third and final dimension is *internal integration,* which refers to the coherent, consistent, interconnected application of HR policy.

As we mentioned in the last chapter, we believe that the first type of integration is the most crucial—the connection between human capital programs and corporate strategy. Within external integration, there are four main connections, according to Mabey and Iles—and confirmed by our experience:

- administrative (purely operational links)
- one way (where HR programs reactively support strategic ideas)
- two way (where there are reciprocal, interdependent links)
- integrative (where there is frequent, dynamic interaction between equal strategic partners)

Each of the connections is necessary, and each one builds on the last. Mabey and Iles call these "links," but this term implies a kind of linear connection, like links in a chain. We experience these connections more as bonds—profound relationships better defined by chemistry than mechanical engineering. (We recall that in chemistry, a bond is a strong force of attraction holding atoms together in a molecule.)

Operational Bond between Programs and Strategy

The operational bond between human capital programs and strategy—a bond occurring through day-to-day business processes—is the most basic program/strategy connection there can be. Without it there can be no strategic fit, just as without molecules there can be no chemical elements. This might be called "fit at ground zero." In Arthur Andersen's terminology, strategy—itself an operating process—must connect to employees as they fulfill the basic operating processes, namely markets, design, production, sales, and invoicing. People have to be taking care of business, so to speak, for the strategy to exist.

To understand the fit between human resources as strategy, one must understand processes—for it is through processes that the connection occurs. This is an area where we as a firm have done a tremendous amount of work. As mentioned earlier, Arthur Andersen has worked with the International Benchmarking Clearing House, a Houston-based nonprofit, to develop a comprehensive list of all the basic business processes. Moreover, using these basic processes as a framework, we have spent the better part of this decade constructing a Global Best Practices™ database to capture what we know about these processes.

We have identified two basic types of processes: operating processes and management/support processes.

When contributing to *operating processes,* managers and others:

- understand markets and customers;
- develop vision and strategy;
- design products and services;
- produce and deliver products and services (manufacturing firms/service firms);
- invoice and service customers.

When contributing to *management and support processes*, managers and others:

- develop and manage human resources;
- manage information resources;
- manage financial and physical resources;

- manage external relations;
- manage improvement and change.

Each of these has many subprocesses—an average of 20 each, hence 260 subprocesses total. Improving the value of human capital requires some sense of all of these basic processes, but three must be highlighted. Expressed very simply, these three are *vision, people,* and *change.* If managers can grasp these three basic elements, they are well on their way to achieving the elusive strategic fit for their human capital programs.

One-Way Bond between Programs and Strategy (Mirroring)

Going one step further now, let us look at the bond between programs and strategy that occurs through mirroring—a one-way, reflective bond in which management and support programs mirror strategy. In particular, we want to look at the way the company *develops and manages the human resources* that perform and support the operational work. This might be called Fit 101.

- Create and manage human resource strategy.
- Cascade strategy to work level. (See Box 9-1.)

BOX 9-1
Cascading Strategy to Work Level

Is our strategy reflected in our:
- recruitment, retention, and retirement?
- rewards and performance management?
- career development and training?
- organizational design?
    outsourcing/insourcing?
    HC function?

- HC enablers?
    legal and accounting compliance?
    employee and industrial relations?
    communications?
    HRIS and other systems?

- Manage deployment of personnel.
- Develop and train employees.
- Manage employee performance, reward, and recognition.
- Ensure employee well-being and satisfaction.
- Ensure employee involvement.
- Develop Human Resource Information Systems (HRIS).

Two-Way Bond between Programs and Strategy

The two-way link is better, as there are reciprocal, interdependent links between HR and strategy. Here we can look more deeply into the potential subprocesses that loop back to strategy. This interlocking might be called "Fit 201." Here are some examples from the Arthur Andersen Global Best Practices™ process list.

When you *create and manage human resource strategy,* be sure to:

- identify organizational strategic demands;
- determine human resources costs;
- define human resources requirements;
- define the organizational role of human resources.

When you *cascade strategy to work level,* be sure to:

- analyze, design, or redesign work;
- define and align work outputs and metrics;
- define work competencies.

When you *manage deployment of personnel,* be sure to:

- plan and forecast workforce requirements;
- recruit, select, and hire the right employees;
- develop succession and career plans;
- create and deploy teams;
- relocate employees;
- restructure and rightsize workforce;
- manage employee retirement;
- provide outplacement support.

When you *develop and train employees,* be sure to:

- align employee and organization development needs;
- develop and manage training and mentoring programs;
- develop and manage employee orientation programs;
- develop functional/process competencies;
- develop management/leadership competencies;
- develop team competencies.

When you *manage employee performance, reward, and recognition,* be sure to:

- define performance measures that align with strategy;
- develop performance management approaches and feedback;
- manage team performance;
- evaluate work for market value and internal equity;
- develop and manage base and variable compensation;
- manage reward and recognition programs.

The remaining areas—ensuring employee well-being and involvement, and developing human resources information systems—must also be linked to strategy in various ways.

Integrative Bond between Programs and Strategy

The integrative link is the best, with frequent, dynamic interaction between equal partners. In this dimension, strategy affects programs, and programs in turn affect strategy. Managers of human capital above all are asked to *manage improvement and change to human capital programs—* the true subject of this book. One might call this "Advanced Fit" or even "Total Fit."

Once again, the Arthur Andersen Global Best Practice™ process list can be instructive. To achieve a fully dynamic interplay between human resources programs and company strategy, managers must:

- measure organizational performance, assessing quality, costs, and productivity among other factors;
- conduct quality assessments based on both external and internal performance;

- improve processes and systems, creating commitment for improvement;
- implement needed programs for change;
- benchmark human capital performance (including, for example, fit with strategy, best practice, and market practice).

FIT IN PRACTICE: A COMPENSATION CASE

Clearly, human capital programs can and must fit strategy at a variety of levels and in a variety of ways. The foregoing discussion has made a strong, if rather theoretical, case for this truth. At this point, though, hands-on managers might be eager to get going in the rough-and-tumble world of actual practice. So now let us turn to an actual case. In this section, we will show exactly how Arthur Andersen, working with a major multinational manufacturer, ensured a fit between its own pay practices and the company's strategy, industry best practice, and market pay levels.

This work in fit grew out of a study of company documents, including the company's annual report, overall business plan, an "HR Direction Plan" it had already developed, and existing statements of vision and mission. It was further informed by discussions with a project management team assembled for the purpose of working with us to conduct a companywide "human capital appraisal." Perhaps the most important insights into fit came from an all-day workshop that focused specifically on the fit between company strategy and compensation. In the workshop, senior managers and other key employees collectively affirmed one primary goal for the company's pay policy, namely to *develop an integrated and coherent rewards policy.*

This strategy, they agreed, should:

- support globalization;
- motivate higher performance, entrepreneurial flair, and customer focus;
- promote teamwork while giving employees a stake in the company's success.

At the workshop, participants assessed strategic fit by ranking cash compensation, pensions, and other benefits against each of these goals. These were recorded as having high, medium, or low fit.

Workshop participants also assessed the best practices fit of these el-

---

BOX 9-2
Three Types of Fit Analysis

	Strategic	Best Practice	Market
Recruitment, retention, and retirement	x	x	x
Performance management and rewards	x	x	x
Career development, succession planning, and training	x	x	x
Organization structure	x	x	—
Enablers	x	x	—

In addition to strategic fit, organizations can determine best practice and market fit. (In the case of organization structure and enablers, market fit is not applicable.) For actual analysis of rewards fit (pensions and other benefits only), see Appendices C(1) through C(3).

---

ements. To do so, they compared the firm's practices to the practices of companies in Arthur Andersen's Global Best Practices™ database, and ranked the company on a scale from innocence, to awareness, to understanding, to competence, to excellence.

Finally, serving as an adviser to the company's managers, we did an independent study of market practices fit, comparing pay levels for key positions against six different studies of pay in the company's industry.

Box 9-2 illustrates the fact that we assessed three types of fit.

ASSESSING THE FIT OF CASH COMPENSATION

Our first area of focus was the company's cash compensation policy. We found a relatively low fit in all areas except for the best practices area, where the company was operating in the higher categories. The section below is our summary of these results (reworded to maintain client anonymity).

Strategic Fit

We found a low fit of cash compensation to overall strategy, because at present the company lacks a fully integrated and coherent pay policy. This could change soon because management is working to correct this lack of alignment.

Cash compensation policies presently do not seem to support the desire for globalization, as the company has no clearly defined remuneration policy for specific grades, either nationally or globally, but there are clear opportunities for improvement.

Again there is a low fit between the compensation policy and the guiding principle of recognizing performance, entrepreneurial flair, and customer focus. . . . Individuals are not really encouraged to take risks, and there is no competence-based pay for the sectors of the workforce where this would be a desirable behavior.

Finally, cash compensation policies do not currently support the desire for team-working. Employees say that there is a focus on the individual in the way people are paid, rather than on team or overall corporate performance.

Best Practice Fit

In assessing the company's fit with respect to best practices, participants agreed that there was awareness or understanding in the cash compensation domain, with the exception of team rewards and equity incentives. In these areas, the group found that the company was still in the stage of innocence.

Participants selected excellence as their goal for the future (defined as two to five years), except in the equity incentives area, however, where competency was set as the goal.

Market Practice Fit

As part of our analysis of the company's rewards system, we also conducted a market comparison of a selection of the company's functional positions—some within the company's industry, and some against multi-industry benchmarks. The twelve positions studied were chosen by the company's project management team and reflected a range of skill types, seniority levels, functions, and locations.

This review shows that in all but two cases, base salary falls within the competitive range expected, albeit on the low end. Despite the high level of compensation paid as a proportion of revenues or total costs, compensation paid per full-time equivalent employee was low. This contrasts with the company's internal belief that it is a median payer.

ASSESSING THE FIT OF PENSION PROGRAMS

Our second area of focus was the company's pensions policy. Here we found a range of fit from high to low, depending on the aspect studied. Here are more excerpts paraphrased from our report.

Strategic Fit

In general, the workshop participants gave a high fit rating to the company's pension plan, recently created through the merger of several smaller ones. Senior managers and key employees felt that this single plan supported a single culture—one of the company's main strategic aims. Fit seemed low with respect to teamwork and stakeholding. Other goals were deemed not applicable to pensions.

Best Practice Fit

In assessing best practice fit, workshop participants and Arthur Andersen looked at benefit design, operation, compliance, value for money (cost of advisers, insurers, and providers), service quality, and administration. The dominant view was that the company's existing pension arrangements show either understanding or competence with respect to best practices. For all pension areas outlined, excellence was chosen as a one-year goal, except for "value for money." In this area, competence seemed an adequate goal over the two-to-five-year range.

Market Practice Fit

In comparison to current market norms in the company's industry, employees have a higher than average range of choices. At the executive "gold" level, contributions are higher than the market norm, but so is the value of benefits.

ASSESSING THE FIT OF OTHER EMPLOYEE BENEFIT PROGRAMS

We also looked at other employee benefits, namely holiday pay, disability pay, private medical insurance, company cars, maternity/paternity leave, and relocation packages. We gave them fit ratings as a group. Here again is a (disguised) quotation from our report.

Strategic Fit

There seems to be a low fit between the company's benefits policy and support of globalization, teamwork, performance, entrepreneurial flair, and customer focus, with no formal policy of discretionary awards to foster these goals. This is not unusual for employee benefits in most organizations.

Best Practice Fit

In comparing the company's employee benefits to our Global Best Practices™ benchmarks, we looked at three aspects: design, administration, and cost of administration. Managers and key employees felt that the company can strive for excellence in all areas except for the cost of administration, where competence is an acceptable future goal.

Market Practice Fit

The company's holiday benefits are generous compared to market trends, except at the senior management level, where they are average. Disability, private medical, and company care provisions are all generous compared to market norms. Maternity/paternity pay is below market norms. Finally, relocation benefits are comparable to the norm.

These thumbnail sketches are based on a far greater level of detail. For illustrations of how we presented the details of strategic, best practice, and market fit in cash compensation, see Appendix C. Our report to the company also included charts for these areas of fit in pensions and other benefits.

CONCLUSION

As we stated in the opening of this chapter, the fit between human capital programs and company strategy must be discovered in the clarification stage, measured in the assessment stage, forged in the design stage, supported in the implementation stage, and checked in the monitoring stage. One way to discover, measure, forge, support, and check the fit of programs to strategy is to consider company processes at the deepest level—both in theory and in practice.

Chapter Ten

ASSESSING HUMAN CAPITAL COST

New Frontiers

Man is the measure of all things.

—Protagorus, *Fragment 1*

In the world of human capital appraisal, cost is king. It is the hardest of the hard numbers managers have, and a magnet for all others. Every manager knows the importance of cost. It is like the "negative" that gives meaning to the "positive"—a kind of antimatter in a material universe. In the creation of net income, there are really only two fundamental operating strategies: maximize revenues and minimize costs. In a sense, cost is one of only three primary numbers recognized by accounting systems worldwide: If business managers know nothing else, they know this—revenues minus expenses equals net income, the "bottom line."

Given the importance of cost in determining value, the managers of human capital obviously need to search hard to find out all human capital costs. Yet to date, very little effort and ingenuity have gone into this critical quest. Companies know what they spend on base pay, bonus pay, incentive pay, and benefits, and they know their overall budget for human resources, but their understanding of human capital cost often ends then and there. Many costs go uncounted, insidiously undermining productivity in myriad invisible ways.

These hidden costs need to be brought to light—not just to know the bottom line for business, but because knowing costs can open up new vistas for managers. As we saw in Chapter 5, cost is a key component in the assessment of programs for human capital management. By considering cost along with fit and value, companies can see whether to cut, maintain, or improve their human capital programs, and whether strategic alignment is required.

How, then, to assess *all* human capital costs—the unseen as well as the obvious? Human resources expert Jac Fitz-enz of the Saratoga Institute, in Saratoga, California, has suggested some new rules of thumb companies might develop.

LABOR COST AND LABOR YIELD

The most common measures of employee cost are *revenue per employee* (R/E) and *pretax income per employee* (I/E). But these ratios are misleading for two reasons. First, R/E and I/E ratios do not differentiate investments in labor from investments in energy, equipment, raw materials, or real estate. Second, traditional employee head count numbers typically count all employees as if they were working full-time on a permanent basis, when in fact a growing percentage of the workforce is working part-time or on a temporary or seasonal basis. Numbers should be adjusted accordingly, with two half-time employees counted as one full-time employee (expressed as a full-time-employee, or FTE, equivalent).

Furthermore, a significant percentage of the workforce is composed of individuals who are not employees—and so may not even show up on an employee head count. This nonemployee workforce includes consultants, contract workers, and leased personnel (some working part-time and temporarily, others working full-time). Again, adjustments are necessary and possible (taking care not to double count if there are separate budgets for nonemployee help). As noted repeatedly in this book, at least half of the workforce in the early twenty-first century worldwide may be composed of such workers.

To take account of these new trends, companies need a new denominator in the R/E and I/E ratios. This number, which quantifies the true cost of all purchased human services, might be called "human expenses." This number (lets call it E_h) would include *all costs* relating to compensation of human services, a figure that includes the cost of full and part-time employees and nonemployees such as consultants and contract workers, as well as the cost of human resources programs. The new benchmarks for the cost of labor are then R/E_h and I/E_h.

To get yield ratio, a company can adjust its adjusted revenues or income by subtracting human expenses, and then using these numbers as numerators and dividing by human expenses. The yield ratio formula would then be AR/E_h or AI/E_h.

PROGRAM COSTS AND PROGRAM YIELD

In Chapter 5, we explained the assessment stage of the Human Capital Appraisal™ process. At that stage—the second in a series of five—managers must assess the fit, cost, and value of various areas within human capital management.

Program Costs

In assessing program costs, we said that managers need to be aware of:

- The *direct costs* of each program, including the costs of facilities, outside providers, and systems, as well as the fixed and variable out-of-pocket hard costs of the program. This can also include head count costs—for example, the cost of an in-house recruiter would be a direct cost of a new recruitment program.
- The *indirect costs* of the program. These may be structural features built into the design or structure of the program, such as the tax consequences of certain forms of retirement savings plans, or they may be "spin-off costs" unique to a program—for example, a high rate of stress-related illnesses triggered by a tough new performance management system.
- The *opportunity costs* of each program, a special kind of indirect cost that includes not only the time employees and their line managers

spend away from their primary jobs because of the programs, but also the lost value of the activities that they might be missing as a result.

Hidden costs can be particularly high when it comes to opportunity costs. For example, senior executives in a firm with a strong pay-for-performance program might spend half of their time making and communicating performance evaluation decisions. Yet this time commitment is rarely counted as a part of the cost of a performance evaluation program. Nor do companies take into account the value of the income the manager might generate if he or she were not evaluating the performance of others.

The field of "systematics" has established that systems, once created, take on a life of their own. Programs and other systems may start up for a perfectly good reason, but they often continue even when that reason is gone. Thus many human capital programs in companies today are running despite little need for them. These programs grow like miniature (and sometimes expansive) bureaucracies, with multiple costs to which managers are resigned. The assessment stage of human capital management—particularly the cost analysis phase of this stage—can help search and destroy, or at least downsize, these unquestioned entitlement programs.

When the true costs of individual programs are known, managers may decide to end them, even if they have names that sound very positive. For example, if a complex "pay for performance" plan is taking up most of managers' time that could be better spent selling and servicing accounts, it may not be worth the amount of true cost it entails.

Program Yield: The Return on Human Capital Index

In assessing not only the cost of programs but their value, it is helpful to plot the fit, cost, and value of each program on a matrix, as shown in Chapter 5. If we take the results from the Fit-Cost-Value™ matrix shown in Chapter 5 and then plot them against benchmarks, we can calculate the Human Capital Effectiveness™ of a company, as discussed in the subsequent chapter on value.

LABOR AS A UNIQUE KIND OF COST: ADVANCED THEORY

Having reviewed the ways managers might calculate the costs of labor and of programs designed to realize the value of labor, let us now turn to the broader vistas of theory. What exactly is cost? What kind of cost is labor? In what ways does labor add value? Is labor a kind of intellectual property? If so, how can its value be protected? Some interesting answers are being developed now in the field of engineering.

One of the main ideas advanced in our book is the notion that expenditures made on employees are not merely sunken costs but investments on which management can expect a return. This leads to the idea of human labor as a form of capital—hence the term *human capital* in our title.

At first glance, it may seem that this use of the term *capital* contradicts accepted cost theory, which makes a sharp division between labor and capital. Indeed, as noted in a recent study by engineering economist Edwin B. Dean, published by the National Aeronautics and Space Administration, economic theory recognizes labor and capital as the two basic (and separate) components of cost.

Dean discusses the separate roles of labor and capital in a series of essays called "Cost Technologies for Competitive Advantage" posted on the Web (http:/akao.larc.nasa.gov). Here's the top line of his message (quoted from the opening paragraph of his executive summary):

Cost is a measure of human endeavor in monetary units. . . . It is an expenditure of resources. These resources include labor and capital. Labor is a measure of human work in units of the total person equivalents applied over time. Capital is a measure of nonhuman resources expended over time. Capital resources include mineral and money rights. So-called capital equipment is not a capital resource since a considerable amount of labor is expended to create it. Capital equipment must be expressed recursively as labor and capital. In other words, the sum of all labor expended to genopersist an object must be accounted for as labor. All other resources expended are accounted for as capital. [Emphasis added.] (Dean 1997)

And further:

> The goal of design is to reduce cost. Thus, successful applications of design for cost result in a negative cost force. That is, they create an acceleration which reduces the power of human endeavor [necessary for an application].

Based on semantics alone, it may seem that Dean is saying labor is no more than a cost that management (and, in engineering, design) seeks to reduce. But let's look further. Dean uses a coined verb, genopersist, which he defines elsewhere as "to bring forth, sustain, and retire an object." In an essay, "Genopersistation from the Perspective of Competitive Advantage," which is part of his aforementioned cost series, Dean explains the levels of this function, as double (when action is taken on an object), triple (when action is taken and an attribute is added), and so forth. *The process of management adds more and more cost and presumably value.*

Dean lists some of the ways in which "genopersistation"—or as we would say, added value—occurs. Human labor adds value by:

- evolving
- conceptualizing
- evaluating
- designing
- producing
- prototyping
- supporting
- testing
- managing
- operating
- marketing
- deploying

In our view, borrowing Dean's term, to genopersist a product is to *add value to it* in all the various ways mentioned—something human beings are uniquely qualified to do. Dean and other leading economists would surely agree then that labor has a *uniquely important role in adding value* and that this role can be quantified and built into sophisticated models of cost using techniques such as activity-based accounting.

To see labor as a cost may seem like a negative way of looking at it, but if we think of cost as an investment that *adds value* and from which one can expect a *return*, then this would mean that labor is a key agent of added value. Design reduces the need for this added value. Design itself, however, is an upfront cost that comes from the expenditure of labor in the form of human ingenuity.

CONCLUSION

Many of the costs of human capital are hidden costs. These costs in fact are investments that may or may not create value. Assessing the true cost of human capital is an important part of determining its value. Thinking about costs with the help of leading theorists, we might say that there are two types—human costs and nonhuman costs. The expenditure of these costs, if well managed, creates value. The human dimension of that value, in our terms, might be called *human capital*. The nature of human capital can be quantified with increasing precision, with cost theory as an important basis.

Chapter Eleven

ASSESSING HUMAN CAPITAL VALUE

The Ultimate Question

And time for all the work and days of hands
That lift and drop a question on your plate.

—T. S. Eliot, "The Love Song of J. Alfred Prufrock"

The value of a human being is arguably infinite, but what is the value of an employee to an organization? What about the value of a management team? Of a workforce? And what about the value of programs designed to enhance that value? Can we quantify these items? These are some of the perennial challenges confronting executives as they seek to realize the value of the human capital they manage.

In the following chapter, having just revisited fit and cost in the previous two chapters, we will return to value, thus completing our closer look at the three basic elements measured in Arthur Andersen's Fit-Cost-Value™ model. We will reveal more about the workings of this model, which (as mentioned previously) plots programs along two dimensions—strategic fit along one dimension, and cost in relation to value along the other dimension. In addition, we will introduce a tool called the Human Capital Effectiveness™ chart. Finally, we will explore the possibilities of accounting for human capital value on company financial statements.

FROM IMPRESSIONS TO INSIGHTS:
VALUE IN THE FIT-COST-VALUE™ MODEL

The poet William Blake once declared that we can find the "world in a grain of sand." This may not be true in an objective scientific sense, but it is true in another important way—a grain of sand contains many valuable clues to the structure of matter in our universe. By the same token, we can gain broad and deep insights into the value of a human capital program at the level of individual employee impressions. Although each individual impression may seem to have only small importance in the big picture (and a subjective one at that), it is arguably the single most fundamental building block of the universe of human capital value.

This is why in the first stage of any new human capital program—the stage we have called clarification—managers need to survey their employees to find out what weight they put on various aspects of a program.

For example, in assessing a training program, a company might send the following questionnaire to its employees, asking them to assess various aspects of the company's training program today and tomorrow, ranking these present and hoped-for future qualities as 5 (strongly agree), 4 (agree), 3 (neutral), 2 (disagree), 1 (strongly disagree).

Questions might focus on the effectiveness of training, its functional relevance, the planning and coordination of the program, the development of skills, the use of new media, and the perceived cost/value benefit to the organization.

Impressions of employees in each of these areas, added together and averaged, can give vital insights into the strengths and weaknesses of a particular program (in this instance training), as well as overall perceived value. Suppose, for example, that the average number in the today column is low, and the average number in the tomorrow column is high. This would mean that employees consider training important and in need of change—hence a potential priority for the organization. If, on the other hand, today's average number is the same as tomorrow's or higher, then the need for change is less compelling.

The last question posed in this questionnaire—indicating perceived value in relation to external benchmarks—may lead to another level of value appraisal that we call "best practices." If questionnaire results show that employees believe the company lags behind its competitors in a particular area, we often undertake this second level of analysis—moving as it were from the subjective to the objective. We characterize the degree of difference as running from innocence (when a company lags in relation to competitors) to excellence (when a company leads in relation to competitors).

Based on the results from employee questionnaires, and based on the questions they themselves have asked and answered during the clarification stage, managers can begin to see the usefulness and administrative ease of the company's various HR programs. They can then compare this value to cost, which gives another indicator for each program. Finally, managers can compare this value/cost number on one dimension to an indication of fit along another dimension—plotting their findings in a Fit-Cost-Value™ model. In Chapter 5, which dealt with assessing the fit, cost, and value of human capital programs, we showed a sample FCV™ chart.

FROM INSIGHTS TO IMPACT: HUMAN CAPITAL EFFECTIVENESS (HCE™)

There remains the larger question of the *return* on human capital investment. That is, when all is said and done, after all the "works and days of hands," as Eliot wrote, does it really pay to invest in human capital? If so, how much? Can the return be measured?

Before turning to the notion of human capital returns in the domain of microeconomics—what happens at the company or organizational level—let us take a tour of macroeconomics, the birthplace of the notion of human capital. (As noted in Chapter 1, the late, great macroeconomist Theodore Schultz is recognized as the "father of human capital.")

To visit macroeconomic landmarks, consult the macroeconomics sections of the book and article bibliographies at the back of this book. From titles alone, it will become quickly evident that *at the national and global level, investments in human capital through education do pay in increased rates of employment and national productivity generally.* The thrust of these studies can be summarized in two quotes from development economists working in Africa and Latin America respectively:

Properly articulated, implemented, and operated, educational and training programs can help develop the necessary human qualities and skills required for economic development. (Abjibolosoo 1996)

Human resource investments are . . . essential for reducing poverty and integrating economic growth and social reform. Investing in people enables work forces to adapt to rapidly changing markets and share in the benefits of economic growth. (Behrman 1996)

If this is true for the whole, should it not be true for the part? Even as nations and international organizations invest billions of dollars in programs for education and training, another equally important process is going on in individual companies all over the world. Large and small, public and private, manufacturing and service, every year, thousands of companies attempt to change the way they manage human capital, devoting substantial amounts of time, money, and energy in the process. Is all the effort worth it? If you have read this far, you must believe that it is—or can be. We share your belief. Based on our own experience as a firm, and based on our clients' experiences, we believe that investments made in human capital programs lead to better financial performance for companies over time—but only under certain conditions. The new program cannot be created in a vacuum, imposed from without, and left to succeed or fail. Rather, it must be interconnected to the very heart and soul of the company—its strategy and its people. Any new human capital program must be

- focused strategically;
- tailored to meet known needs;
- shaped by the views of the people it will affect;
- realized through organizationwide commitment;
- tracked against strategy.

In the previous chapters, we have shown a process for meeting these requirements—namely the stages we call clarification, assessment, design, implementation, and monitoring. If companies follow a process like this one, they will meet the most important goal of organizations today—the enhancement of human capital.

In each of the five stages, an organization needs to cover all aspects of the company's human resources management. To review these areas once more, the first and most fundamental area relates to movement: recruitment, retention, and retirement. The second is the closely related area of performance management and rewards. Next comes career development and training. A fourth area is organizational design. The fifth and final area requiring management attention is the broad realm of what might be called human capital "enablers"—systems for improving legal compliance, employee and industrial relations, communications, and information flow. Chapter 12 shows how companies around the world are improving the nature and allocation of their investments in these areas—all with good results.

In Chapter 1, we concluded by citing studies that show superior returns for companies that make investments in their human capital. We also cited evidence that institutional investors are beginning to place their capital in companies with a good human capital profile. The U.S. Department of Labor has an intense and continuing interest in the connection between labor practices and return-on-equity investment, one of the themes sounded by Labor Secretary Alexis Herman in a March 31, 1998, speech at the Council of Institutional Investors in Washington, D.C.

Nor is this attitude confined to the United States. In the United Kingdom, the Royal Society for the Encouragement of the Arts (RSA) has proposed that a new type of corporate personality must emerge. "Tomorrow's Company" will make a concerted investment in its human capital, predicts the RSA, which urges investors to invest accordingly. The RSA's call for human capital investment has met with an affirmative response by several major investors.

Consider the mission statement of Kleinwort Benson Investment Management, a European institutional investor committed to investing in companies with a high human capital profile. In this statement, Kleinwort Benson says that it positively values companies that invest heavily in training and people. In doing so, it uses a scorecard that rates companies for several elements. At the very top of the KB checklist, there is the imperative for management to "develop a success model."

We believe that managements *can* develop success models for human capital in their companies—and use these models to improve financial performance. In organization after organization, we have seen real improvements in classic financial indicators—such as sales, profits, and stock value—after management has focused on human capital. These improvements are measurable. In the previous chapter on cost, we have shown some simple rules of thumb (R/E_h, I/E_h, AR/E_h, and AI/E_h). Managers can use these numbers as rough indicators to see what kind of returns they are getting on the true cost of labor.

In addition to these ratios, managers can measure the effectiveness of their human capital programs against other companies' programs. For example, the results from a company's Fit-Cost-Value™ analysis may be benchmarked against the FCV™ findings from other companies. These results may be plotted in a Human Capital Effectiveness™ chart, as shown in the following chart.

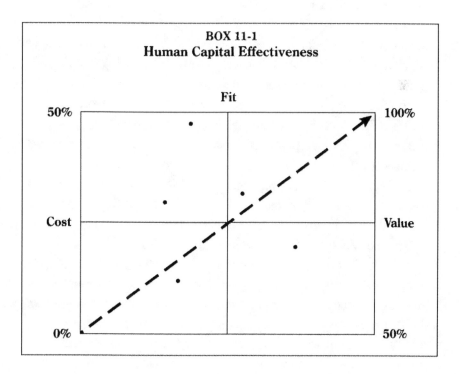

BOX 11-1
Human Capital Effectiveness

We hope that this and other tools for appraisal introduced throughout this book can be important success models for managers of human capital. The only great challenge remaining is how to account for this value in public financial statements.

THE ACCOUNTING CHALLENGE

Therefore, in closing our chapter on value, it is high time to look at the accounting challenges raised by all of the foregoing. The question is: How does all this compute to the income statement and balance sheet? In Chapter 10 we already saw some techniques for better cost accounting. This is certainly a good beginning. The serious works in the field tend to focus on costs—from Eric G. Flamholz's classic *Human Resource Accounting* (1985) to Janice and Ahmed Monti-Belkaoui's *Human Resource Valuation: A Guide to Strategies and Techniques* (1995). The Monti-Belkaouis offer some very practical ways for putting human resource investments on financial statements.

This recognition for literal accountability through accounting actions is long overdue. The profound idea of nonmonetary capital is sweeping the globe. We read about "social accounting" for internal and external humanitarian programs at companies like Atlantic Richfield and Eastern Gas & Fuel Associates (Monks and Minow 1995). And we marvel at the brilliance of insights on "intellectual capital" from Thomas A. Stewart (1997), a *Wall Street Journal* veteran, and from Leif Edvinsson (1997), director of intellectual capital at Skandia, one of Europe's most respected and forward-thinking financial firms. We learn about accounting for "natural capital" from the environmentalists and even about "emotional capital" from industrial psychologists such as Kevin Thomson (1997). Can these values be put on financial statements?

Thomson writes in *Emotional Capital* that "assets like passion, obsession, motivation, desire, innovation, and knowledge will be critical in creating the products, services, and relationships which produce lifetime loyalty from customers and colleagues alike." Thomson predicts that "within five years emotional capital will become the accepted measure of success. It will be an asset on every business balance sheet. It will be reflected in the stock price as a tangible, hard measure of soft issues." Thomson explains that "intellectual capital may be the currency of the organization, the words people use to trade and to build up stocks of value from what it thinks, knows, and uses. But unless organizations can harness and nurture their beliefs and passions intellectual capital is worthless."

This kind of thinking certainly is inspiring—almost a call to arms in the war against inadequate accounting. Yet as accountants, we believe in evolution, not revolution. So ideas like Thomson's send us back to basics, not forward to battle (not yet anyway). And in going back to basics, we go back to the beginning—asking, what is accounting for value anyway?

In the very first research study it ever published, the American Institute of Certified Public Accountants defines accounting as follows:

- To measure the resources held by specific entities.
- To reflect the claims against and interests in those entities.
- To measure the changes in those resources, claims, and interests.
- To assign the changes to specifiable periods of time.
- To express all of these things in terms of money as a common denominator.

This raises questions for the human capital notion. Can we say that employees are "held" by the entities that employ them? What kind of claims are there against employees, and what kind of interests are held in them? How can one measure changes in the value of a company's workforce and in the claims and interests they may generate? How can we set a time frame for this measure? And, finally, how can we express these things in terms of money? These are the questions that confront forward-thinking managers and accountants today—and the subject of our planned sequel to this book.

CONCLUSION

How can companies account for human value? Answering this question is difficult but not impossible. Clues abound, and we must keep gathering them—traveling a long, hard road before we answer these questions. As we noted in our opening chapter, changes in accounting standards do not happen overnight. But companies can begin accounting for human capital in a voluntary, "off-balance-sheet" manner. Remember, generally accepted accounting principles set forth *minimum* standards of disclosure and the rules for meeting these standards; they do not preclude the introduction of other measures. The human capital measurement tools we set forth in this book can be used in this regard.

Chapter Twelve

HUMAN CAPITAL

The Road Ahead

The future enters into us, in order to transform itself in us,
long before it happens.

—Rainer Maria Rilke, *Letters to a Young Poet*

S tage by stage, area by area, tool by tool, the preceding pages have
brought managers through a top-level overview of how to enhance
the value of human capital. We have shown readers how to move
through the Human Capital Appraisal process and its five stages of clarification, assessment, design, implementation, and monitoring—focusing always on the areas of human capital that need improvement.
Managers who have applied these lessons along the way already know
what we do: A strategy-driven process applied to change in the human
capital area can lead to significant, positive change over time. This certainly has been the experience of the hundreds of managers around the
globe who have tried this approach.

In this final chapter, it seems appropriate to tell a little more about the
experience of the companies we know who "realize the value of people."
First and foremost, of course, are the anonymous companies whose programs we described in previous chapters. But these companies, while
exemplary, do not stand alone. There are many more firms that know
how to "realize the value of their people."

This chapter offers brief vignettes of the human capital practices that over thirty companies developed using some or all of the change-management processes advocated in this book. For our U.K. cases, we relied heavily on "Managing Best Practice: The Regular Benchmark" publications, a subscription-based series of reports published by the Industrial Society of the United Kingdom (telephone (44) 121 454 6769). The cases have been cited with the kind permission of the companies concerned. Each case study is referenced in the bibliography, under sources for Chapter 12, with the relevant edition information. We also referred to studies by Income Data Services (IDS), a research group that provides pan-European income information.

Our U.S. cases are based on information contained in Arthur Andersen's proprietary Global Best Practices database. We are grateful to our colleagues Robert Hiebeler, Thomas B. Kelly, and Charles Ketteman for drawing them to our attention.

These cases are by no means exhaustive. We also know of exciting and effective initiatives in a variety of industries, including broadcasting (BBC) express services (Federal Express Logistics), processed food (Cadbury-Schweppes), restaurants (TGI Fridays), to name just a few. But although we did not have the space or time to include a comprehensive list of cases, we hope the following "snapshots" capture the kind of programs companies can build in their search for higher returns on human capital.

Not all of these companies are Arthur Andersen clients—and of the Arthur Andersen clients, not all of these companies have worked directly with our Human Capital Services practice. Nonetheless, we offer them here as a way to show managers the kind of results that can be accomplished if companies seek to invest in their human capital.

These stories take seconds to read—but they took months and even years to evolve. For, to repeat the ancient wisdom cited earlier in this book, "it takes a long time to bring excellence to maturity."

BEST PRACTICES: HUMAN CAPITAL INITIATIVES

How do other companies achieve a high return on human capital? There are no paradigms, since every company has unique socioeconomic and business circumstances. Moreover, few companies measure the return on their investments in human capital, and even fewer publish their findings. There is, however, a large body of evidence (mentioned in previous chapters) that indicates that various best practices in human capital can lead to better financial performance. The following case studies show some of the actions various companies are taking to improve the value of their human capital.

Recruitment, Retention, and Retirement

One of the most basic human capital functions is of course *recruitment* to fill open positions in an organization.

- At the multibillion-dollar **BT plc,** an entire division is devoted to the recruitment of college graduates. The unit acts as a consultancy to the main divisions within BT to ensure that recruiting efforts target needed skills. The personnel director of each of the divisions makes bids to the unit based on past trends and expected developments. The recruitment process is undergoing continual improvement, as managers solicit feedback from recent new hires and adjust the program accordingly. Initial screening is carried out by the computer to ensure that only candidates who meet requirements are considered for openings. All candidates are briefed on activities they can expect throughout the recruitment process. BT also has a post-recruitment *mentoring* program that supports the company's commitment to *diversity.* As part of the company's broader mentoring program, BT has one for women mentoring women, as well as networking opportunities for ethnic minorities.
- At **Land Rover Vehicles,** part of the multibillion-dollar German car manufacturer **Daimler-Benz,** interviews occur during a comprehensive recruitment day. The day involves a variety of aptitude tests as well as a group exercise that gets all candidates to work together on a project to reveal teamwork and communication skills. Candidates are able to present themselves in a variety of situations designed to put them at ease. The company tries to involve as many current staff as possible.

- **Tesco,** a multibillion-dollar food retailer with presence in England, France, and Hungary, offers prerecruitment training designed to tackle programs such as lack of confidence or poor interview techniques. This enables the company to fulfill one of its strategic goals—to hire employees that represent demographic trends in areas surrounding stores. The candidates who are recruited tend to be more motivated and are more likely to stay on and succeed in the company.

- **Fingerhut,*** a multibillion-dollar U.S. catalog company, is an AA client who learned in the process of clarifying its goals that it was committed to reaching the Spanish-speaking market. It decided to commit itself to recruiting Hispanics and actually moved its telemarketing operations to southern Florida in order to do so—a classic case of good implementation proverbially known as "bringing Mohammed to the mountain" (instead of the other way around). For more about companies with asterisks, see Robert Hiebeler, Thomas B. Kelly, and Charles Ketteman, *Best Practices: Building Your Business with Customer-Focused Solutions* (New York: Simon & Schuster, 1998).

- Last but not least is the example of **Mobil Oil Corp.*** The $71 billion multinational oil company worked with our firm to improve its customer service, and found that recruitment was a problem area—one that had a poor fit with strategy. The company was looking for people who knew how to operate a cash register, hoping they would be friendly. In a change of approach, it decided to recruit friendly people, and, if necessary, teach them how to tote numbers.

Performance Management and Rewards

In clarifying their strategy and assessing current programs, many companies decide that they need to institute new programs for *flexible benefits*. Although the cost of administering a flexible benefits program is higher than the cost of a traditional program, it can increase employees' commitment and motivation.

- **Colgate-Palmolive,** the U.K. branch of the $9 billion U.S. global consumer products company, decided to give permanent, salaried staff the chance to control and adjust their individual benefits as part of a broader empowerment scheme. Instead of imposing a system, the company formed focus groups where employees discussed what benefits they might want and how much they would be willing to pay for them. Under Colgate's flexible benefits plan, employees can contribute up to pre-defined legal limits, with an increase or decrease in take-home pay depending on benefits chosen. In implementing the new plan, Colgate set up a computerized administration system. Also, it maintained continuous communications (reminding employees of the program), as well as continuous review and improvement of program offerings and administration.

- At **Cutler Hammer,** * a privately held supplier of automobile and industrial parts based in Pittsburgh, the company decided to link merit pay increases to the meeting of objectives in a team setting. (For more examples of teamwork, see following under performance management.) Team objectives were expressed in terms of specific targets for revenue growth and customer satisfaction. The rewards philosophy has led to steady increases in both.

- At **Royal Mail,** the U.K.'s postal service, management introduced flexible benefits for all employees with personal contracts. The new program started after the company formed a group of managers and other employees to discuss benefits issues, and found that the current benefits did not reflect the needs and values of the employees. After consulting with an outside adviser, the company created a database to generate communications and process employee choices. After the company started the new program, it continued to solicit employee reactions. These regular reviews have revealed widespread acceptance of the new program.

Performance management has been the focus of many human capital leaders. The following two examples can serve as a prelude to this extremely important area.

- Continual performance improvement was a key focus at the **Chicago Tribune,** the privately held U.S. newspaper company. The company conducted a complete review of all the human capital programs for its newspaper sales force, including recruitment, rewards, performance management, and training, as well as organization structure and various enablers such as communication. As a result of this assessment, the company decided that it needed a complete shift in culture—from a hierarchical, seniority-based culture to a results-oriented, competency-based one. One of the many changes the company instituted was a program to recruit the kind of people envisioned for the "new" Chicago Tribune. (See Box 12-1.)

- Performance management includes *task management*. At the U.S.-based hotel chain **Ritz-Carlton Hotel Company,*** a subsidiary of W. B. Johnson Property, Inc., this is down to a science. The only hotel chain to ever receive a Malcolm Baldrige Award, the Ritz-Carlton stipulates that every Ritz-Carlton hotel compile daily reports covering 720 work-related tasks. Hotel managers measure, for instance, how much time housekeepers need to clean a room. This helps the company set reasonable expectations for job performance, neither demanding too much nor too little of its people.

The journey from clarification to monitoring has brought a number of companies to a decision to use *360 degree evaluation* for performance management, sometimes linked to rewards.

- **One-2-One,** a multimillion-pound U.K. mobile telecommunications company, requires all managers to use 360-degree evaluation, but makes it less threatening by deliberately detaching it from performance review and salary results—using it instead as an adjunct to career development.

Another relatively new practice in performance management is the area of management *competencies*—the behavior patterns that the incumbent needs to bring to a position in order to perform its tasks and function with competency (Boam 1992).

- **The Body Shop International,** a multimillion-dollar global retailer of skin and hair products based in the United Kingdom, identifies core competencies to review people's performance. The company wanted greater precision in the terms it used for learning and development—and it found the use of competencies helpful in this regard.

BOX 12-1
Toward a New Culture: Chicago Tribune

Many companies wait until their financial performance plummets before they consider new strategic directions, and when that happens they turn to outside consultants for the answers. The **Chicago Tribune** defied both conventions when it decided to change its strategic course during a time of prosperity—and to consult its own employees on how to do it.

During this recent period of transition, the multibillion-dollar media and entertainment company owned what was arguably the most successful newspaper in America—the *Chicago Tribune*—one of the world's most profitable major metropolitan newspapers. The sales force of this century-old institution continued to bring in a steady flow of advertising dollars, benefiting themselves and the rest of the staff. The "Trib," as it was affectionately called, was widely considered a good place to work.

In such positive circumstances, other managers might have decided to pursue business as usual, but not the senior managers of the Chicago Tribune—all was not quiet on their midwestern front. They worried that the flow of dollars for newspaper advertising could dry up if advertisers chose other media, such as radio or television. To be sure, the Trib owned radio and TV stations, but they wanted to prevent those lost news-ad dollars from going to competitors. So they convened the Trib's news-ad sales force for a series of "vision" sessions to clarify the company's future.

With the help of facilitators, the salespeople formed a long-term strategy for their own efforts, identified barriers to achieving this strategy, and removed these barriers by redesigning various human capital areas—notably recruitment, organization structure, and compensation.

- In the past, the company had consistently hired steady, service-minded, security-oriented performers, and had rewarded them through generous base pay and bonuses. In their strategy sessions, the salespeople saw that they really needed to have two groups of salespeople. In the new Chicago Tribune, there would still be a group of salespeople devoted to providing excellent service to existing customers in return for stable rewards through base pay and bonuses. But the new Trib, to be built up through recruitment, would also employ a more aggressive type of salesperson to land new business in return for commissions—with a very high upside potential. To use an image from prehistoric times, the company would have not only "gatherers" but also "hunters."

- The introduction of these new "hunters," the salespeople knew, would topple the old seniority system, which had distinct levels of status and pay based on time spent at the company (the "trainee" received the least pay and the "senior sales associate" the most, with various levels in between). In the new Trib, performance would determine pay for all salespeople to a greater degree, with the greatest risk built into the pay of the "hunters." With the help of facilitators, the salespeople also urged a new cross-selling approach to pay: They said they wanted to receive financial rewards not only for selling newspaper ads, but also for referring business to the radio and TV parts of the company. The company instituted a new position called "media consultant" to help clients develop strategic media plans. This new position would focus on selling all the Trib's media—not just print.

- At **Eastman Kodak,** the U.S.-based $19-billion leader in photographic imaging, the entire workforce was screened to identify potential team leaders who were then sent on to a further two-day assessment program. Chosen team leaders then attended seven weeks of training over a 21-week training period. Training continued with appraisal, counseling, and monitoring of employees over the next nine to 24 months. Finally, the Kodak Certificate in Team Management Skills was awarded to team leaders who underwent a management assessment project.
- **H.J. Heinz,** a $9.4 billion U.S.-based global food company, restructured its management in response to heightened competition. Team leader roles were advertised internally and were open to all employees. Team meetings are now held regularly to ensure that all teams are fully aware of the role that they play in the achievement of business objectives. Also, upward appraisals (subordinate appraisals of bosses) have been introduced as a team-building activity.

Many companies provide inspiring examples of another performance management tool—*empowerment*. The following five companies are particularly exemplary.

- Empowerment means little without power, and there is no clearer expression of power than budgetary authority. This is a secret of success for the multibillion-dollar **International Business Machines (IBM)** company in motivating its workforce and linking employees to customers. In some parts of IBM, managers have implemented a "Customer First" initiative (which could also have been called "We Trust Our People") that gives each frontline employee the authority, without prior management approval, to spend up to five thousand dollars per incident to solve problems for a customer on the spot.
- At the chemicals division of **British Petroleum,** a multibillion-dollar multinational corporation engaged in the exploration, production, transportation, processing, and marketing of oil and gas, an empowerment program began in an effort to promote competitiveness. In the mid-1990s the company created a cross-functional team to examine the way tasks were being carried out in the company to see how

tasks previously done by groups might be accomplished by individuals. Key features included a structured communication system (team briefings at the beginning of every shift and group meetings every month); formal training and an open learning center on site to foster multiskilling; creation of self-regulating, multiskilled teams who decide their own pace of work; and, last but not least, individual rewards based on the individual's skills.

- At **Stamco,** a subsidiary of the multimillion-dollar U.S.-based **Monarch Machine Tool Company,** management became aware that it had a hierarchical "blame" culture rather than a competency-based learning culture, so it instituted a number of changes, including daily meetings to cover immediate issues; monthly performance feedback sessions; reduction of strict departmental boundaries; and removal of status symbols such as parking spaces and company cars. This has led to increased profits over the past three years.

One important aspect of the empowerment movement, as the examples above show, is *teamwork.* Here are some best practice companies in this regard.

- At the privately held **Robert Bosch GmbH,** * the world's leading supplier of electronic automobile components, with many billions in annual sales, there are cross-functional teams of employees who "own" all manufacturing and distribution processes. These teams oversee the entire production and supply-chain processes from start to finish.
- In the early 1990s, **Holy Cross Hospital*** of Chicago was in the bottom 5 percent of hospitals nationwide, as rated by the Press-Ganey Patient Satisfaction Index of 440 U.S. hospitals. A few years later, it had moved to the top 5 percent. The difference was teamwork. The hospital created "Commando Teams" made up of employees throughout the hospital to identify and correct any problems experienced by "customers" (patients and their families and friends). The fifteen hundred staff members, called "partners," got involved in quality details—and moved the hospital up 80 points in patient surveys within a single year.

Yet another program in the performance management arena is the new trend toward *flexible working arrangements* for employees. These arrangements include *part-time* work; *flextime* that lets employees choose (within limits) how to arrange the hours they work; compressed workweeks, a variation of flextime; *job sharing*, through which two employees share the pay and the responsibilities of one job; *multiskilling*, which expands the skills of employees and permits more task and even job rotation; and *telecommuting*, or letting employees work from locations away from the company office. After assessing their human capital management programs, several companies have decided to explore this kind of program. Here is one story in brief.

- **BP Chemicals,** the chemicals division mentioned above for its empowerment initiative, wanted to instill a culture of continuous improvement and flexibility among job roles. As an adjunct to its mid-1990s empowerment initiative, the company decided to create cross-skilled production teams in tandem with a skills-based pay structure. BP makes annual payments to employees who have progressed through prescribed skill levels. Also, the company has created production teams, deemphasizing the reporting hierarchy in favor of a focus on safety, skills, and the needs of the business, not job roles. In another feature of the program, employees are given free time that they can use to increase their skill levels.

Yet another area we have worked in is *job evaluation.* The following two companies have accomplished great things in this area.

- **Ericsson Ltd.,** the UK subsidiary of a Swedish telecommunications firm, has connected its job evaluation scheme to the responsibilities and competencies that are considered the most valuable in the firm. To conduct evaluations, the company used a computer program based on competence, rather than a discretionary system created by existing managers. This helped the company avoid a common trap of evaluation schemes, which often merely mirror an existing hierarchy. The new evaluation approach enabled the company to use the same system for evaluating technical and managerial roles (formerly segmented). In all phases of launch, the company had a high level of employee participation through both written and verbal communications. The competencies are freely available to employees, who can use them for career development and planning. Also, the system is fully integrated with other HR initiatives at the company.

- The mission of **Unilever plc,** a branded foods company with billions in worldwide sales, is to provide a working environment within which employees can fulfill their potential. The company uses a job evaluation panel to reduce individual bias. Panel membership is balanced between men and women, to ensure gender neutrality in the system. One strength of this program was employee communication during the design and implementation stages.

Career Development, Succession Planning, and Training

For a good example of *career development* and *succession planning,* one need go no further than the **Royal Bank of Scotland.** (See Box 12-2.)

At the multibillion-dollar multinational pharmaceutical firm **Glaxo Wellcome,** a coaching program began when the company went through a broad-scale change in culture. The company launched a two-part program—one part for the sales force out in the field, and the other part for the head office. Key features of the program included senior management involvement, creation of teams with a diverse range of people, and integrating coaching into daily efforts.

Three clever training ideas (all very good examples of capturing the intellectual capital within human capital) can be seen in the following examples.

- At **Sarcom,*** a privately held information technology company in Columbus, Ohio, the company asked its most customer-focused employees (the ones winning all the prizes for customer service) the secret of their success. The employees all had similar answers, which essentially involved six steps. The company wrote up these six steps and distributed them on plastic cards to all employees!
- At the U.S.-based **Hyatt Hotels,*** a multibillion-dollar hotel chain, management relies on customer surveys to develop a best practice database that is used for training employees. Each month, a cross-functional team led by Hyatt's senior vice president of operations takes up critical guest concerns and creates a "best practices list" to

---

BOX 12-2
Career Development In-Depth: Royal Bank of Scotland

Royal Bank of Scotland, a billion-pound banking and financial services organization, has established assessment and development centers to help employees plan their careers at the company. These centers help generate personal development plans for each individual. These plans are linked to the company's business goals. The bank formalized the program in the 1980s and restructured it in the early 1990s to be more closely aligned with business needs and the current industry market. Individuals are encouraged to "own" and develop their own careers.

The bank's career development program arose from a visioning session in 1992 in which managers set out to become "the best financial services group in the U.K. by 1997" and to maintain the bank's lead through career development. Managers envisioned that "by 2000, 85 percent of our staff will have a relevant professional or vocational qualification." Today, five years later, they are still committed to that vision. Overall, the company is trying to foster a culture of ownership, accountability, and empowerment in which all staff members feel responsible for their own results and company results, and the processes used to achieve those results.

Highlights of the program include:

- *Regular formal coaching and feedback.* The individual's immediate manager has the role of coach and becomes the visible symbol of the firm's interest in the individual's growth and development. Managers hold dialogues with individuals to discuss performance (in the individual's current role) and career development (for the individual's future role(s). A personal development plan is drawn up after the two discussions.
- *The personal development plan.* In this plan, employees identify the competencies and skills they wish to develop, the actions they wish to take, and the results they hope to achieve. The employee chooses from a list of forty competencies identified by the bank as useful to its business. After envisioning developmental activities, the employee may request support, and suggest a timetable—including the timing of future reviews. Each employee discusses the plans with his or her manager, who approves the plan (with any necessary amendments).
- *Development resources.* Developmental opportunities within the bank include: an open learning environment, computer-based training, multimedia training, task forces and project teams, and programs for coaching, mentoring, and shadowing.

---

meet them. Every hotel in the Hyatt system receives a copy of each best practice for distribution to every employee.

- The humorously named **New Pig Corporation*** (a privately held manufacturer of industrial absorbents based in Tipton, Pennsylvania) has an unusual way to link senior management, employees, and customers. Customer service calls are often monitored by New Pig executives, who work with the phone reps to glean useful information from each call. Company president Nino Vella periodically undergoes customer service training and takes customer calls to keep the knowledge fresh.

Organizational Structure

Organizational structure is often slow to change, unless managers deliberately attempt to change it. One way to change an organizational structure is to strive to create a *learning organization*—one that continually transforms itself by instilling in its employees a willingness to change and adapt. A learning organization, which often has a "flat" organizational structure with very few management layers, focuses on creating, acquiring, and transferring knowledge and modifying behavior to reflect this knowledge. Here are some notable learning organization pioneers.

- During a time of intense competition in the oil industry, the North Sea unit of the aforementioned **Mobil Corp.** decided to break down its work processes into tasks and analyze them—benchmarking against competitors whenever possible. The process and the results were discussed at employee forums in order to share knowledge. As an outgrowth of this phase, the company created multidisciplinary learning teams, as well as learning rooms for self-directed learning, learning workshops to share learning, and regular off-site strategy sessions.

HC Enablers

One important enabler is, of course, the *communications* function.

- Again, the U.K. branch of **International Business Machines (IBM),** the computer manufacturer mentioned earlier for its empowerment program, uses communication advisers to deliver the communication strategy for each of its internal business units. The company employs a broad range of face-to-face channels such as business manager meetings, management roadshows, and executive visits. Upward communication is strongly encouraged. The company has a "Speak Up" program, through which anonymous views can be sent to Speak Up coordinators who send the message on to the appropriate person.

Some companies have decided to focus on the *communication of suggestions.*

- **BT plc,** mentioned earlier for its recruitment and competency programs, introduced a "New Ideas" scheme as part of a quality program. Employees pass suggestions to the relevant manager, who may act on ideas directly, or who may pass them on to a central coordinator who enters the details into a database. The relevant division then receives the suggestion, and will act on it within a time limit of between thirty and seventy days, depending on the impact of the suggestion. The employee making the suggestion receives regular feedback on progress. If the suggestion leads to cost savings, the employee may receive a cash award ranging from \$41.75 to 5 percent of the saving, with a limit of \$41,750. BT pays any tax due on awards.
- At **Vauxhall Motors,** a U.K.-based subsidiary of the multibillion-dollar **General Motors,** an "employee recognition" plan is open to all employees up to middle management. Supervisors are instructed to encourage ideas from employees, and are expected to deal with around 70 percent of these themselves. The remaining, more significant, ideas are sent to a coordinator who can award cash payments of up to \$20,040 subject to approval by a senior manager. A points system is in place to score and reward suggestions—not only those that lead to cost savings, but also those that provide an intangible benefit. Each employee receives a plan booklet when joining the company. The personnel director, senior coordinators, and recognition officers meet every few months to review the operation of the scheme.

Another important enabler is a good information system (human capital information system, or HCIS).

• In this arena, **Norrell Corporation,*** an Atlanta-based temporary services agency, is exemplary for its link to quality. Norrell's quality measurement system, called IRIS (for integrated research information system), generates a survey after each assignment to measure the Norrell employee on a scale of one to five in ten dimensions. A central database at the company's corporate office scans the feedback from customers and generates reports measuring quality by branch, customer, and employee. Four out of every ten customers fill out the survey. Managers then use this feedback to evaluate, reward, and coach employees.

CONCLUSION

In reading these stories, readers may wonder why we waited until the end of our book to introduce these success stories. Why not the beginning? The reason is simple: human nature. When managers see a success in the next company over, they naturally want to copy it. Imitation may be the highest form of flattery, but it is not the way to effect meaningful change. We would be rich if we had dollars for every time a client came to us and said, "ABC Co. has a great program. We want one too"— but we always decline such work.

Even if it means losing a consulting assignment, we always ask our clients to resist the impulse to emulate—and instead to step back and look at the big picture, to clarify. What do you *really need?* Is it a program like that one, or might it be something else? Or are you fine the way you are? This approach takes time, but it has served us and our clients in the long run. Change is an inside job; it *must* come from within. In order to realize the value of the human capital at your company, you as a manager must go through your own processes of clarification, assessment, design, implementation, and monitoring.

As we bring this book to a close, it seems right to return to the instructive realm of parables. In our opening chapter, we drew a lesson from the biblical Parable of the Talents, drawing this simple lesson: Companies that have good people need to invest in them. Now, in closing, we can learn from Parable of the Sower (see Box 12-3).

BOX 12-3
The Parable of the Sower

A sower went out to sow his seed; and as he sowed, some fell on the path and was trampled on, and the birds of the air ate it up. Some fell on the rock; and as it grew up, it withered for lack of moisture. Some fell among thorns, and the thorns grew with it and choked it. Some fell into good soil, and when it grew, it produced a hundredfold.

The cases in this chapter show how the "seed" of a new human capital program, planted in "good soil," can bring abundant success to a company. In our view, the good soil needed is not a physical location, but rather a management process—one that can help you increase the value of human capital at your company "a hundredfold."

EPILOGUE

"Rags to riches" stories ring true to managers around the globe. We all want to confirm our hope that wherever markets are free, an individual human being can move from the ghetto to greatness in a single generation. This is the ultimate value migration. But the movement from poverty to wealth for individual human beings can only happen when people have a positive yet realistic view of their own potential. This great migration of human capital value happens not only for people individually, but also collectively. Just as individual people can accumulate wealth, so can organizations—if they can appraise, manage, and leverage the value of the people they employ. As we enter the new millennium, this is the *ultimate challenge* for managers—realizing the value of their people by transforming human resources into human capital.

How can we make this bold claim? How can we say that people are supremely important—more important today than money or technology? Some might accuse us of preaching a gospel that few practice—or, more starkly, perpetrating the "biggest lie in contemporary American business," to quote Michael Hammer again.

We hope that our book has demonstrated that human capital is no myth, but a very real fact of economic life. Furthermore, we hope that we have convinced the reader that human capital is valuable and can be valued. In closing, we would add the assertion that human capital is the *preeminent component in the value of any organization.*

Our reasoning begins with the simple fact that financial and technological capital depend entirely on human capital, whereas human capital depends on little if anything beyond itself. Money and technology can create nothing without people, but people can go far with almost nothing but the basics of survival—coupled with a strong will to survive and provide.

THE PREEMINENCE OF HUMAN CAPITAL

Beyond this basic truth, there are many emerging trends that point to human capital as the single most important issue facing all types of enterprises today. Around the world, in both the private and public sector, and in profit-seeking and nonprofit enterprises alike, human capital is rapidly ascending in importance when compared to financial and technological capital.

One reason that human capital has jumped to the top of our priorities is the classic rationale of *supply and demand*—an issue of particular importance in the private, for-profit sector, but also relevant in other domains. Put simply, money and new technology are abundant today, while skilled human capital is scarce and growing scarcer.

- With the growth of worldwide markets for equity and debt capital, financing has become relatively easy to obtain. Given a decent plan, virtually any entity—be it a company, a country, or a cause—can obtain the money it needs to operate. Therefore, being well capitalized financially cannot ensure survival in any competitive domain.
- A similar phenomenon is unfolding in the realm of technology, where the market for new ideas is flooded daily—causing a paradigmatic shift in each basic technology at least every eighteen months, experts say. It is very easy to replicate an existing technology, so it is very hard to compete on that basis.
- By contrast, human capital, which takes a long time to produce, has become a precious commodity. This is true not only for skilled labor "out there" in the marketplace—everyone knows about the supply-side crisis there—but also *within* organizations. It takes a long time to build up the way a company's people learn and build together. This

forms a significant part of a company's value. When companies down-size, merge, or otherwise restructure, these systems go through up-heaval, and human capital value can be lost. Human capital value dissipates not for the simple fact that individual employees walk out the door—human capital is more than people. Rather, this loss of value occurs as organizations lose their effective teams and productive cultures—or fail to build them.

In addition to this basic economic fact, several additional trends are con-spiring to raise the importance of human capital. One such trend is an *aging population and workforce,* and a decreasing ratio of workers to re-tirees, especially in major developed countries such as the United States. Another trend is the critical *shortage of technical workers* needed to solve the Year 2000 problem. Yet another is the growth in part-time and contract workers. As discussed in the opening chapters of this book, all these trends clearly point to the importance of human capital.

FACING THE FUTURE

Given the fundamental importance of human capital, and the many cur-rent trends that are increasing this importance, what can managers do? This book has offered guidance on how to manage human capital through various stages and in all its areas, including recruitment, retention, and retirement; performance management and rewards; training, develop-ment, and succession planning; organizational structure; and "enablers" such as communication and regulatory compliance. Arthur Andersen is in the knowledge business. As such, our most valuable asset is our people. As a result, we invest heavily in our human capital. For example, Arthur Andersen has a world-class college recruitment program to hire the best and brightest. We now invest over 6 percent of our gross in-come on training.

We also provide tools, technology incentives, and accountability mechanisms to share knowledge on a global basis. Investing in training is one of the best ways to enhance the value of human capital in compa-nies—and in nations. (Indeed, the term "human capital," as we noted in our opening chapter, is heavily associated with national education and training as a way to empower individuals, enhance growth, and reduce poverty.) At Arthur Andersen, we believe very strongly that organizations can reap rewards from wise investments in their human capital, and we take every possible occasion to put our belief into words—including the words of this book.

But actions speak louder than words. That is why we have decided as a firm to invest a significant portion of our financial, technological, and human capital in the building of a Human Capital Services practice. We believe that the tools we teach in this practice, such as Human Capital Appraisal™ and Fit-Cost-Value™ can bring the notion from promise to reality. Ultimately, we hope to develop a comprehensive metric that can be used to rate the effectiveness of human capital in organizations—both for the organizations and for their shareholders.

We will call this new metric the Arthur Andersen Human Capital Index™. It is our hope that this index, in combination with the tools we have already developed, will become an important resource for directors, senior managers, investors, and others. In a sequel to this book, we will reveal more about this emerging metric. Meanwhile, we hope to join you on the road ahead—as you chart the course of human capital in companies now and in decades to come.

Appendix A

Case Studies

CLARIFICATION

In 1997, Arthur Andersen began to work with a leading multinational to review its HR strategy, policies, and procedures to align them with the company's strategy and values.

The company's strategy covered seven points:

- Becoming the world's best.
- Giving people the freedom to act.
- Developing employees to their full potential.
- Maintaining a strong financial base.
- Finding the most cost-efficient solutions.
- Becoming the partner of choice around the world.
- Facing the future with confidence and integrity.

The company's values also covered seven points (each supported by HR guiding principles developed later by Arthur Andersen):

- Leading by example. (Develop leadership by means of personally demonstrated values.)
- Good communication. (Create an open and honest culture for employee involvement.)
- Working as a team. (Encourage teamwork to break down professional barriers.)
- Managing and developing potential. (Establish career management and succession planning for all and state-of-the-art recruitment and training processes.)
- Rewarding performance. (Emphasize pay for performance.)
- Encouraging learning and innovation. (Create an environment where best practices, knowledge, and ideas are shared.)
- Empowering staff. (Give employees the ability and authority to achieve results.)

How well was this company prepared to practice what it was preaching? The following case study summarizes the lessons learned.

Initial Work

Initial work involved context-setting in advance of a detailed scrutiny of the company's human capital policies and its newly intended strategy. We involved a wide range of employees in this phase, including senior managers and key staff, in order to secure their participation, ownership, and support for the implementation of change later on. All too often, new programs are developed by well-meaning HR departments only to gather dust months later for lack of wide support.

In this stage, we interviewed senior managers and key decisionmakers face-to-face, and sent an attitude survey to employees' homes with a personalized cover letter. We used a structured interview template for the interviews to ensure consistency and comprehensiveness. Through the interviews, we hoped to gain an understanding of the business and strategic issues facing the organization, and to determine each stakeholder's role with respect to those issues.

Following the interviews and the questionnaire mailings, employees were asked to participate in interactive interviews via "keypad" sessions facilitated by Arthur Andersen. These confidential sessions were designed to boost response rates and made use of an alternative and novel surveying medium. The technology allows audiences to quickly answer questions presented on a large screen and to receive instant graphical feedback of audience responses. In order not to duplicate the employee survey questions, the keypad sessions focused on more HR-related issues.

We introduced the keypads late in the planning process in response to the HR department's concern that the response to the employee attitude survey would be low. Typically, employee surveys attract a response rate of 30 to 40 percent; therefore, the HR client team was keen not to risk being embarrassed by a low response rate.

The thirty-minute sessions, which took place at various company locations, proved very popular with employees. The events provided the HR client team with an additional communication mechanism with which to position and explain the context of the HR review. As such, the events provided multiple communication opportunities. The sessions were advertised by posters and were deliberately kept short and punchy to provide an opportunity for brief but professional introductions from HR line managers.

In reality, the fear of a low response proved to be unfounded. Responses to the employee attitude survey reached 63 percent. The response to the keypad sessions was also high, with 52 percent of staff attending the sessions. According to a 1994 study by the Industrial Society of the United Kingdom, only 14 percent of organizations ever achieve these levels of response rates.

Reporting on Questionnaire Results

Feedback—reporting back to staff—is a critical feature of any survey process, and this one was no different. All client staff received a feedback report containing color graphics of the compiled company responses to questions from both the employee survey and the keypad sessions. An executive summary, produced by Arthur Andersen, drew out the main findings and conclusions.

Findings from the employee keypad survey were generally positive. A full 90 percent of employees said they were proud to work for the company. However, some findings showed less congruency:

- 56 percent would be willing to leave, or might consider leaving, for no net gain in the financial package. (Employees with two to five years of service were the most likely to leave for no financial gain.)
- 52 percent said they were not completely satisfied with their reward packages.
- 48 percent believed that communication between departments is poor.
- 46 percent of employees did not understand current business goals.

Checking these results and many more against the company's stated goals, we found some gaps between goals and achievements. In other words, the company's intentions were not always realized in its actions—despite its best efforts. We used the survey results to grade the company's level of success in living each of its values, focusing on several areas.

Case Study Summary

Stage 1 is predominantly focused on assessing the current state of an organization and preparing the ground for change. A key factor is real participation. Management is not merely making employees "feel" a part of the change process. The employees' views will help build that process. The payoffs are twofold—a better plan, and better acceptance of the plan. Staff and senior managers are more likely to support this kind of approach to change as opposed to an alternative where change is recommended behind closed doors.

In our opinion, nine elements contributed to the success of Stage 1 for this client:

- Care in deciding the best survey approaches.
- Comprehensiveness of survey questions.
- Confidentiality of survey results.
- Senior management awareness of the problems and issues likely to arise from the survey.
- Senior management commitment to act on the findings.
- Emphasis on communication and involvement.
- Effective use of technology.
- Fast and objective feedback to staff.
- Use of consultant as facilitator—not "expert."

For the client, the stakeholder interviews, the employee questionnaire, and the keypad interviews helped the HR team identify the key issues and to position the new strategy within the business context while achieving high levels of staff involvement: 84 percent of employees voted in support of management's decision to review its human resources programs—a clear mandate for moving on to Stage 2, assessment.

ASSESSMENT

The previous section focused on the clarification stage of our work (Stage 1). This section now continues with highlights from work we did in the assessment phase (Stage 2).

To recap, in the clarification stage, we identified several issues and gaps between the company's stated goals and actual achievements.

Then, in the assessment stage we carried over our findings on the lack of strategic fit to take a closer look. We wanted to see how well the human resources programs of the company aligned with not only strategy but operations. After reexamining *fit*, we also looked at *cost* and we looked at *value* in relation to cost. Using our Fit-Cost-Value™ approach to appraise this company's human capital programs, we:

- measured the fit of human capital programs in supporting the company's culture and business objectives;
- calculated the cost of these programs;
- improved the value of these programs.

Working with senior management in the client company, we identified the following HR processes for review within the client organization:

- *Recruitment* (with emphasis on orientation)
- *Rewards* (base pay, incentive compensation, and benefits)
- *Career development* (with emphasis on succession planning)
- *Global organizational structure* (with emphasis on expatriate assignment policies)

In the assessment stage, we performed a Fit-Cost-Value™ analysis of the company's HR policies and processes. The diagram summarizes the key elements of the approach.

Fit-Cost-Value™

- Measuring the **fit** of human capital programs in supporting an organization's culture and business objectives.
- Calculating the **cost** and improving the cost-efficiency of these programs.
- Measuring and improving the **value** of these programs in the eyes of the employee.

The following core HR processes were identified for review within the client organization:

- Pay and benefits
- Recruitment and induction
- Career development and succession planning
- Training and development
- Expatriate assignment policies

Other processes were also examined but were not subjected to a full FCV™ analysis. These include performance management and HR information systems. Each element of the process is examined in detail below.

Fit

This part of the process involved assessing how the HR strategy and its component policies and benefits fit with the business strategy and with current best practice.

- *Business Strategy Fit.* Assessing business strategic fit involved identifying the key areas of the client's business vision and strategy. In practice, this proved a difficult task due to the absence of a clearly articulated and communicated business strategy. The information that was available was not, as is the case in many organizations, in a readily accessible form. Various sources of data were, therefore, pooled to piece together a picture of strategic intent and core values. Sources included: annual reports; business strategy documentation; anecdotal comments and "soundbites" from directors and senior managers, along with inputs from the employee attitude survey. This provided a rich and comprehensive database of qualitative information from which to "deduce" the organization's strategic intent, core values, and beliefs. The core values and beliefs were used as the basis for defining the HR guiding principles or vision statements with the client.

  In assessing business strategic fit, each of the five HR process areas was evaluated against the business strategy, values, and beliefs, and guiding principles. Fit was assessed as high, medium, or low, with supporting evidence. From this it was possible to identify and prioritize the changes required to current policies and processes in order to align them more closely with the business strategy.

- *Best Practice Fit.* To assess best practice fit, a model was constructed of specific best practice behavioral examples anchored to a five-point scale. The scale ranged from "innocent" at one extreme to "excellent" at the other. Best practice definitions were developed for each of the subprocesses of the HR functional areas. For example, recruitment was comprised of the following subprocesses, for which best practice examples were developed: candidate/job specification; communication of vacancy; marketing of opportunities; selection.

An "innocent" organization might, for example, have no formal interview-record forms or process, whereas an "excellent" organization may be one that has a clear process that is meticulously documented. Examples of best practice were developed using the Arthur Andersen Global Best Practice™ database and other external library sources.

Matrices were developed that defined the company's current position but also identified the actions required to achieve the desired future level of competence. It should be noted that in some cases the organization may not want or need to achieve an excellent rating in a given area. The purpose of the exercise is to identify the organization's current position, its target, and the gap between the two in order to develop action plans to close the gap. For more on fit, see Chapter 9.

Cost Analysis

Using standardized and predefined cost templates, discussions were held with key representatives of the HR function and other interested parties to establish the direct and indirect costs of their key HR processes.

Costs were divided into:

- *Direct costs* incurred in supplying the HR service, such as HR department payroll costs, recruitment agency fees, training course costs, consultancy fees, etc.
- *Indirect costs* such as cost estimates of the HR resources and time required to manage/provide the various HR procedures and processes.

Costs when available were compared with benchmark data to establish potential opportunities for cost savings. It became clear fairly early on that in many cases accurate cost data was not instantly available and in some cases was not available at all. For example, information on training costs was not available due to the fact that training was highly decentralized and records were not in a consistent format or kept in any one place. These findings, in themselves, illustrated the need to introduce better controls and processes for collating and tracking key data.

In some cases a cost analysis was not conducted because the HR process could not be expressed in quantitative terms, for example, career development. For more on cost, see Chapter 10.

Value Analysis

The aim of the value analysis was to identify the current perceived value and future perceived value to the employee of specific HR policies/benefits, or components thereof, within the organization.

We defined "value" as the balance of worth and importance to the employee (as he or she would like it to be) relative to their personal and work circumstances (current perceived situation). The objective of the exercise was to identify the value gaps, *i.e.*, those HR policies and processes that were perceived not to be adding value and which, therefore, needed to be addressed as a matter of urgency.

The assessment of "value" was based on information obtained through discussions with HR representatives and a cross section of senior management; the employee attitude survey and keypad findings were also a valuable source of information.

Value Analysis: Checklist for Expatriate Program

(On a scale of 1 to 5, with 5 meaning "strongly agree")

Today		Like It to Be
2	A. The selection process for assignments should be fair and open, and family and individual circumstances fully considered to appoint the best person.	5
3	B. The company should ensure that my family and I are adequately prepared for the assignment. There should be few surprises awaiting us that could have been foreseen.	5
	C. ...	
	D. ...	

In one phase of our study, we focused on the company's expatriate program. (See box.)

We collected data in this area and others, and then analyzed the data using the "value gap analysis" method, which identifies the gap between the current perceived value of the HR policy/ benefit/process and the expected value that the employee would like to get from it in the future. The current and future values were then plotted onto a HR values identification grid, which presented a two-dimensional summary view of the findings. (See the grid on the following page.) A similar model can be used to analyze trade-offs between cost and value. (See Box 5.1 in Chapter 4 on Assessment.)

The following is an interpretation of the ratings:

- Improve or eliminate: indicates processes that will require attention in the long term.
- Improve: indicates processes that should be addressed immediately and that are vital to the success of the organization.
- Hold or eliminate: indicates processes that are of little importance to the organization.
- Maintain: indicates processes that are seen as strengths, because the organization has attained or nearly attained the level of competence required.

Using the Results of the FCV™ Assessment to Develop an HR Strategy

The power of the FCV™ approach rests in combining the outputs of the fit, cost, and value analyses to identify and prioritize the areas requiring action. In some cases there will be contradictory evidence that needs to be addressed. For example, in the case study the value analysis revealed that employees said they were very pleased with their expatriate package—this would seem to indicate that there is no need to change it in any way. However, the cost analysis revealed that the rates being paid were vastly uncompetitive compared with other benchmark companies. The fit

HR Values Identification Grid

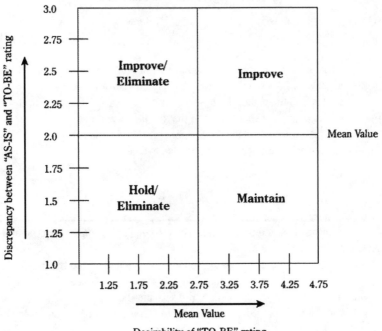

analysis also revealed that the process of selecting candidates for international assignments was perceived to be unfair and did not fit with the core value of fair access to development. Taken together the outputs indicate clearly the areas that the HR strategy would need to address.

Conclusion

The *process* of conducting the Fit-Cost-Value™ exercise itself was very powerful, highlighting significant opportunities for the client. The *outputs* were also key in identifying areas of weakness, particularly in the areas of career development and performance management (e.g., performance measurement and reward systems) that needed to be addressed immediately. To counterbalance this, strengths were also identified in other areas such as in the recruitment processes. An important finding was that the HR department needed to establish better processes for collating and tracking its key costs.

It is always difficult for an organization to undergo an assessment or audit by an independent and external third party. The very process itself implies some way that an organization is unable to manage its own affairs and therefore requires external help. Addressing the negativism and defensiveness associated with the process is a key challenge. It is important to explain at all times why particular data is required and where it fits into the bigger picture to enable the HR team to feel part of the process.

Ultimately the purpose of conducting the FCV™ analysis is to identify opportunities for improvement and development—it is not a backward-looking exercise that focuses on all that is wrong in the organization but a forward-looking one that explores ways of adding value and making a difference in the future.

Implementation Worksheets
for Twelve Initiatives

This section features twelve sample implementation worksheets with fictional results from a hypothetical FCV™ process. These examples have been included in
order to help deepen understanding of this approach. The worksheets can help companies implement initiatives for all five main human capital areas—specifically for
the following subareas:

- recruitment
- cash compensation
- pension design review
- pension plan operations development
- review of employee benefits package
- performance management
- career development and succession planning
- training and development
- expatriate program
- teamwork
- learning organization
- employee communications/input

Each sample checklist shows *key tasks*, *provisional timescales*, *costs*, *impact*, and *ease*.

Initiative Name: Recruitment

Description:
Review and redesign all aspects of recruitment, including manpower planning, induction, and equal opportunities to streamline the process.

Key Tasks:	Provisional Timescales Months			Cost (in thousands of dollars)
	0-6	6-12	12-18	
• Centralize recruitment responsibility in one department.	■			
• Streamline recruitment process and policy (HR/line responsibility, standardized forms, candidate communications, develop 2-year manpower plan, including graduates).	■			
• Develop database of job descriptions and person specifications.	■			
• Develop recruitment referral plan.	■			
• Develop database of candidate CVs.		■		
• Provide interview and selection training.	■			
• Develop recruitment pack for candidates.	■			
• Develop detailed induction pack linked to department induction.	■			

Work required to introduce initiatives:	Approximate External 3rd-Party Costs:
In-House ✔ | **External 3rd-Party** ✔ Both: % In House 75% % External 25%	Insert fees/expenses.

Impact for Achieving Business Strategy:			Ease of Implementation:		
High	Medium	Low	High	Medium	Low
	✔			✔	

Initiative Name: Cash Compensation				
Description: Overhaul grading and salary policies, roll out cash- and equity-based bonus programs and recommunicate benefits to employees.				

Key Tasks:	Provisional Timescales Months			Cost (in thousands of dollars)
	0-6	6-12	12-18	
• Review and revise annual bonus arrangements, extending the more developed structures at board level.	■			
• Redesign current grading and salary policies to include: — competency focus — broad bands to replace existing grades.		■		
• Consider expansion of equity-based opportunities, e.g., highly leveraged arrangements.	■			
• Launch new initiative on communication to increase perceived value of equity incentives.	■			
• Improve communication to line management on market positioning.	■			
• Explore scope for nonmonetary incentives and key contributor awards.	■			

Work required to introduce initiatives:	Approximate External 3rd-Party Costs:
In-House ✔ **External 3rd-Party ✔** Both: % In House 20% % External 80%	Insert fees/expenses.

Impact for Achieving Business Strategy:			Ease of Implementation:		
High	Medium	Low	High	Medium	Low
	✔			✔	

Initiative Name: Pension Plan Design Review				
Description: Determination of strategy for pension provision resulting in new plan design to meet business objectives.				
Key Tasks:	**Provisional Timescales Months**			**Cost** (in thousands of dollars)
	0-6	**6-12**	**12-18**	
• Conduct an internal assessment of strategic needs and current options.	■			
• Assess current and projected market trends.	■			
• Develop design options, including pros/cons and transitional issues.	■			
• Consult with trustees and external providers.		■		
• Refine plan design and finalize.		■		
• Complete implementation planning.		■		
• Communicate plan changes internally and externally.		■		
• Complete implementation.		■		

Work required to introduce initiatives:		Approximate External 3rd-Party Costs:		
In-House ✔	**External 3rd-Party ✔**	**Insert fees/expenses**.**		
Both: % In House 75% **% External** 25%*				
*This will change dramatically if the company decides to move to a defined contribution or hybrid defined benefit plan.		**Transition costs will be lower if the existing defined benefit plan is retained.		
Impact for Achieving Business Strategy:			**Ease of Implementation:**	
High	**Medium**	**Low**	**High**	**Medium**	**Low**
	✔			✔	

Initiative Name: Pension Plan Operational Developments

Description:
Improvement of operational aspects of pension plan to improve value for money and ensure sufficient control and oversight.

Key Tasks:	Provisional Timescales Months			Cost (in thousands of dollars)
	0-6	6-12	12-18	
• Review existing consulting/administration arrangements. • Determine appropriate split of internal vs. external expertise. • Tender third-party consulting/administration arrangements. • Implement any changes in consulting/administration arrangements, including appropriate mechanisms for monitoring external providers. • Recruit or re-train staff to increase in-house expertise.	███			

Work required to introduce initiatives:	Approximate External 3rd-Party Costs:		
In-House ✔	External 3rd-Party ✔	Insert fees/expenses.	
Both: % In House 50% % External 50%			

Impact for Achieving Business Strategy:			Ease of Implementation:		
High	Medium	Low	High	Medium	Low
		✔	✔		

Initiative Name: Review of Employee Benefits Package

Description:
Carry out a general review of employee benefits package to determine the cost/benefit of introducing a flexible benefits program, and introduce such a program if appropriate.

Key Tasks:	Provisional Timescales Months			Cost (in thousands of dollars)
	0-6	**6-12**	**12-18**	
• Conduct feasibility study looking at flexible benefits — obtain Board/HR and employee views — determine proposed plan design — financial modeling — address other issues relating to existing benefits, e.g., cost issues. • Implement flexible benefits (if appropriate) and other changes to benefits package — finalize plan design — contact benefit and service providers — train internal staff, as applicable — prepare and distribute plan.	■	■		

Work required to introduce initiatives:	Approximate External 3rd-Party Costs:
In-House ✔ **External 3rd-Party** ✔	**Insert fees/expenses*.**
Both: % In House 20% **% External** 80%	*General ballpark figure. Actual costs will depend on the extent of involvement in each stage of the process and the actual design of the plan.

Impact for Achieving Business Strategy:			Ease of Implementation:		
High	Medium	Low	High	Medium	Low
	✔			✔	

Initiative Name: Performance Management

Description:
Redesign the performance and career development review to create a process that is competency- and objectives-based.

Key Tasks:	Provisional Timescales Months			Cost (in thousands of dollars)
	0-6	**6-12**	**12-18**	
• Establish 100% completion of assessments as a key management goal.	▉			
• Cascade business objectives to all staff.	▉			
• Develop objective-setting workshops for employees and managers.	▉			
• Implement rigorous tracking processes.		▉		
• Introduce coaching training.		▉		
• Introduce voluntary 360-degree appraisal.		▉		
• Introduce performance-related pay such as a bonus program.	▉			
• Develop competencies for all roles that are aligned to business strategy.	▉			

Work required to introduce initiatives:	Approximate External 3rd-Party Costs:
In-House ✔ **External 3rd-Party** ✔ Both: % In House 30% % External 70%	Insert fees/expenses.

Impact for Achieving Business Strategy:			Ease of Implementation:		
High	**Medium**	**Low**	**High**	**Medium**	**Low**
✔				✔	

Initiative Name: Career Development and Succession Planning				
Description: Develop a robust career development and succession planning process that is fully integrated with the performance management process and training and development initiatives.				

Key Tasks:	Provisional Timescales Months			Cost (in thousands of dollars)
	0-6	**6-12**	**12-18**	
• Develop a career development policy and process.	■			
• Develop a database of skills.	■			
• Introduce a succession planning process.	■			
• Introduce personal development plans as part of the appraisal process.		■		
• Introduce learning and development resource center, e.g., library or Website.	■			
• Implement mentoring and coaching program.	■			
• Redesign process for internal transfers to be consistent with new career development policy.	■			

Work required to introduce initiatives:			Approximate External 3rd-Party Costs:		
In-House ✔		**External 3rd-Party ✔**			
Both: % In House 40% **% External 60%**			*Insert fees/expenses.*		

Impact for Achieving Business Strategy:			Ease of Implementation:		
High	**Medium**	**Low**	**High**	**Medium**	**Low**
✔				✔	

Initiative Name: Training and Development

Description:
Create a separate training and development function to manage individual training and development plans, coordinate management development programs, and other training initiatives.

Key Tasks:	Provisional Timescales Months			Cost (in thousands of dollars)
	0-6	6-12	12-18	
• Create a separate training and development function.	■			
• Develop a training directory of key courses for each job function.	■			
• Introduce development needs training for managers.	■			
• Introduce a senior management development program.		■		
• Conduct training needs assessment and evaluate training effectiveness.	■			
• Implement coaching and mentoring training for managers.	■			
• Develop learning environment.			■	
• Introduce teamwork training initiatives.		■		

Work required to introduce initiatives:	Approximate External 3rd-Party Costs:
In-House ✔ **External 3rd-Party** ✔	
Both: % In House 40% **% External 60%**	Insert fees/expenses.

Impact for Achieving Business Strategy:			Ease of Implementation:		
High	Medium	Low	High	Medium	Low
✔				✔	

Initiative Name: Expatriate Program				
Description: Reengineer international mobility management program to move to best practice and achieve significant cost savings.				

Key Tasks:	**Provisional Timescales Months**			**Cost** (in thousands of dollars)
	0-6	**6-12**	**12-18**	
• Process-map current policy and procedures.	■			
• Survey current and past expatriates.	■			
• Evaluate current tax strategy.	■			
• Reengineer and redraft current policies and processes.		■		
• Determine HR software requirements.	■			
• Determine and implement tax minimization strategy.		■		
• Evaluate allowance and premium levels providers.	■			
• Engineer communication strategy for introducing changes.		■		
• Review effectiveness/appropriateness of changes.			■	

Work required to introduce initiatives:	**Approximate External 3rd-Party Costs:**
In-House ✔ **External 3rd-Party** ✔ **Both: % In House** 30% **% External** 70%	*Insert fees/expenses.*

Impact for Achieving Business Strategy:			**Ease of Implementation:**		
High	**Medium**	**Low**	**High**	**Medium**	**Low**
	✔			✔	

Initiative Name: Teamwork				
Description: Foster a teamwork environment and implement means of eliminating barriers to teamwork.				

Key Tasks:	Provisional Timescales Months			Cost (in thousands of dollars)
	0-6	**6-12**	**12-18**	
• Introduce teamwork training initiatives to break down professional barriers. • Share knowledge. • Ensure performance rewards recognize team contributions.	■	■		

Work required to introduce initiatives:	Approximate External 3rd-Party Costs:	
In-House ✔	**External 3rd-Party** ✔	
Both: % In House 70% % External 30%	Insert fees/expenses.	

Impact for Achieving Business Strategy:			Ease of Implementation:		
High	**Medium**	**Low**	**High**	**Medium**	**Low**
✔				✔	

Initiative Name: Learning Organization

Description:
Become a "learning organization" by sharing knowledge and processes to enable the organization to constantly transform and adapt to new circumstances.

Key Tasks:	Provisional Timescales Months			Cost (in thousands of dollars)
	0-6	**6-12**	**12-18**	
• Establish knowledge-sharing processes and culture.		■		
• Introduce a knowledge-management system on the company intranet.		■		
• Train staff to access and share knowledge.		■		
• Introduce a learning and development resource center, e.g., a library or Website.	■			
• Explore distributed teamwork/ flexible work.		■		

Work required to introduce initiatives:	Approximate External 3rd-Party Costs:
In-House ✔ **External 3rd-Party ✔** **Both: % In House** 30% **% External** 70%	Insert fees/expenses.

Impact for Achieving Business Strategy:			Ease of Implementation:		
High	**Medium**	**Low**	**High**	**Medium**	**Low**
✔				✔	

Initiative Name: Employee Communications/Input

Description:
Undertake communications to ensure that staff fully understand the business and HR strategies and the impact that these strategies have on them.

Key Tasks:	Provisional Timescales Months			Cost (in thousands of dollars)
	0-6	6-12	12-18	
• Communicate business strategy to employees, e.g., video/roadshow. • Develop a plan for the communication of the HR strategy and rollout including as a priority: — communication to increase perceived value of equity incentives — communication to line management on pay market positioning — initiative to address low morale. • Introduce an employee suggestion program. • Introduce employee work councils.	■	■		

Work required to introduce initiatives:	Approximate External 3rd-Party Costs:
In-House ✔ | **External 3rd-Party ✔** Both: % In House 75% % External 25%	Insert fees/expenses.

Impact for Achieving Business Strategy:			Ease of Implementation:		
High	Medium	Low	High	Medium	Low
✔				✔	

Pensions: Strategic, Best Practice, and Market Fit

The following charts show how Arthur Andersen presented the results from an assessment of strategic, best practice, and market fit. Some terms and results were changed to ensure client anonymity.

STRATEGIC FIT: PENSION PROGRAMS

VALUES AND BELIEFS	GUIDING PRINCIPLE	HIGH	MED	LOW	N/A	EVIDENCE (to support your assessment)	SOURCE (survey or personal contact)
		ASSESSMENT OF FIT					
Ensuring fairness and consistency of terms and conditions by creating a single coherent and integrated culture.	Develop an integrated and coherent pensions policy.		✔			High fit has been assessed as one single pension arrangement, which has been developed from integrating a number of plans.	Company focus groups
Promoting globalization and creating a culture of shared commitment to company business objectives.	Develop pensions policy to promote business objectives and ensure employees have a stake in the company success.			✔		Some pension plan arrangements would provide a link with company success. For example, profit sharing and employee stock ownership plans can provide a direct link. In addition, making monetary contributions in the form of employer securities can also be used to link employee and shareholder interests.	Company focus groups
Developing a responsive, customer-focused organization geared to customer satisfaction, quality, growth, and adding value. Fostering taking responsibility and initiative, and being entrepreneurial but remaining accountable for results.	Design pensions policy to recognize performance, entrepreneurial flair, and customer focus.			✔		See above.	Company focus groups
					✔	No direct way of linking.	
Developing a strong teamwork ethic, encouraging open communication and cooperation with knowledge sharing.	Support teamwork culture through pensions systems.				✔	No direct way of linking.	Company focus groups

BEST PRACTICE FIT: PENSION PROGRAMS

Note: Following our assessment, we have shaded chart areas to show current vs. future desired position.

	Benefit Design	Plan Operation	Compliance
I n n o c e n c e	• The existing plan no longer meets corporate or employee needs. • The company considers pension plan design unimportant and does not consider it worthwhile reviewing or changing.	• Trustee body is ineffective due to lack of effective training and coordination.	• The plan and/or its management may not be in full compliance with pension laws and regulations.
A w a r e n e s s	• The existing plan has been in place for many years and has not been reviewed for some time. • The company is aware of the need for a review of pensions policy but prefers to wait until it is forced to do something due to competitive or employee pressure.	• Trustees meet occasionally to consider problems and issues as they arise (i.e., reactive).	• Trustees and other key parties have a basic level of knowledge and understanding but have received no training. • Trustees and other key parties are aware of the legislative requirements for the plan.
U n d e r s t a n d i n g	• The plan design is intended to address the basic corporate and/or employee needs; however, this has not been assessed in many years.	• Trustees and other key parties meet regularly but infrequently to discuss relevant matters.	• Trustees and other key parties have received basic training to help carry out their duties and have a fair level of knowledge and understanding. • Trustees and other key parties aim to ensure legislation is complied with.
C o m p e t e n c e	• The plan design is appropriate and in line with industry standards, although it does not meet all the company's and/or employees' objectives. • The plan reviews take place from time to time to assess the extent to which the plan meets the needs of the company and its employees.	• Trustees and other key parties meet regularly and frequently to discuss relevant matters.	• Trustees and other key parties have had training and have reasonable knowledge and understanding of pensions matters. • Trustees comply with legal requirements.
E x c e l l e n c e	• The plan is well designed to meet the needs and objectives of both the company and the employees. • The plan is frequently reviewed to ensure it continues to meet the needs and objectives of both the company and employees.	• Trustees and other key parties have a high standard of plan governance.	• Trustees and other key parties have a good knowledge and understanding of pensions issues through regular and comprehensive training.
C o m m e n t s	• The plan design is appropriate and in line with industry standards, although it does not meet all the company's and/or employees' objectives. • The plan reviews take place periodically on an ad hoc basis to assess the extent to which the plan meets the needs of the company and its employees.	• Generally the plan appears to operate fairly smoothly with the trustees and other key parties performing their duties reasonably well.	• There have been many changes to the pensions area in recent years and it is necessary now, more than ever, to ensure that trustees are adequately trained to oversee the plan properly, that the providers of services to the plan provide good value for money, and that the service provided to the members is of a high quality.

	Value for Money of Advisers, Insurers, and Providers	Quality of Service	Plan Administration
I n n o c e n c e	• Service and value for money from advisers, insurers, and providers are never reviewed.	• Members receive poor service.	• Administration arrangements are ineffective and systems outdated. • The department provides poor quality service to its customers. • Costs are very high relative to performance and service levels. • Procedures, processes, and performances are never reviewed.
A w a r e n e s s	• Service and value for money from advisers, insurers, and providers are reviewed infrequently.	• Members receive a marginal level of service.	• Administration arrangements can cope with operational requirements but are slow and inefficient in producing results. • Administration would benefit from a structural review of procedures and processes. • Costs are high relative to performance and service levels. • Procedures, processes, and performance are seldom reviewed.
U n d e r s t a n d i n g	• Advisers, insurers, and providers are reviewed occasionally to assess levels of service and value for money.	• Quality of service to members is adequate.	• Administrators deal inadequately with the administration of the plan. • Costs are reasonable in relation to performance and service levels. • Procedures, processes and performance are reviewed from time to time.
C o m p e t e n c e	• Reviews of plan advisors, insurers, and providers are carried out from time to time to assess levels of service and determine value for money.	• Members receive high quality service.	• Administrators are efficient and effective on the whole, although standards can slip from time to time. • Costs are low in relation to performance and service levels. • Procedures, processes, and performance are reviewed regularly.
E x c e l l e n c e	• Procedures are in place for regular review of advisers, insurers, and providers, in terms of the level of service and value for money.	• Members receive high quality service at a reasonable price.	• Administrators provide a quick, effective, and quality service, with a customer-oriented focus. • Administration procedures and processes are continually under review to ensure they are effective and up-to-date. • Performance of administrators is regularly reviewed to assess efficiency both internally and externally. • Overall, administrators provide good value for money.
C o m m e n t s			• As the administration of the plan is carried out by a third party, it is essential that the fees charged be competitive and that the service provided be at appropriate levels. If you are paying for a service you should demand the best. This requires periodic monitoring by an interaction with the company. • Key issues here are turnaround times, accuracy of information provided, and clarity of communication material.

MARKET FIT: PENSION PROGRAMS

Benefit Description	Employees		
	Typical Benefit Levels		Company Benefits
Plan type	Defined benefit	Defined contribution	Defined benefit
Normal retirement age	65 for all	65 for all	65 for all
Pensionable salary (PS)	Basic salary	Basic salary	Basic salary
Final pensionable salary	Average of last three years pay	N/A	Career average pay
Postretirement increases	*Ad hoc*	N/A	*Ad hoc*
Employer's contributions	Balance of Cost*	5-15% of pay	Balance of Cost*
Members' contributions	2.5% of pensionable salary	Variable	Up to 15% of pay
Pension accrual rate	$1/40^{th}$–$1/66^{th}$	N/A	$1/50^{th}$
Benefits on separation from service	Joint & survivor annuity	N/A	Joint & survivor annuity
Contracted-out Status	Contracted-out	Contracted-out	Contracted-out

Benefit Description	Executives		
	Typical Benefit Levels		Company Benefits
Plan type	Defined benefit	Defined contribution	Defined benefit
Normal retirement age	60 for all	60 for all	Varies 60 - 62
Pensionable salary (PS)	Basic salary	Basic salary	Basic salary (for most)
Final pensionable salary	Last 12 months PS	N/A	Average of last three years of pay
Pension increases	CPI	N/A	CPI
Employer's contribution	Balance of Cost*	15–30% of basic salary	Balance of Cost*
Members' contributions	None	Variable	None
Pension accrual rate	$1/30^{th}$	N/A	$1/30^{th}$
Contracted-out status	Contracted-out	Contracted-in	Contracted-in

*Subject to prescribed minimum and maximum statutory funding standards

Pensions: Cost Analysis

A Sample Worksheet

CASH COMPENSATION

DIRECT COSTS $ $

Fixed Compensation

    Salary
    Temporary employee salary costs
    Other contractual fixed allowances
    Call-out pay   _____

    Total Fixed

Variable Compensation

    Performance-related pay
    Overtime
    Shift allowances/ shift bonuses
    Other cash-based incentive payments   _____

    Total Variable   _____

TOTAL DIRECT COSTS   _____

Temporary Employees

Temporary employee costs represent monies paid directly to agencies, and as such are an additional material cost to the company and have been brought within the cost template and benchmarking undertaken later in this report.

PENSION COMPENSATION

The following section sets out the direct costs to the company associated with its main pension plan. The indirect costs of the main plan are included in the next section, on remuneration as a whole.

DIRECT COSTS	Cost as % of pensionable salary	$
Pension Benefits Accrual (current and post-service costs)		
Pension Plan Benefits (other than death benefits)		
Average In-Service Death Benefits		

Expenses
    Costs of administering plan
    Fees for professional advisers (actuary, lawyer, accountant)
    Miscellaneous fees and taxes

Less Employee Contributions

Surplus Amortization		———
TOTAL DIRECT PENSION COST		———

OTHER BENEFITS

DIRECT COSTS	Cost as % of pensionable salary	$
Vacation		
Disability income		
Life insurance		
Health insurance		
Dues and subscriptions		
Auto allowance		
Other		
TOTAL DIRECT COSTS OF OTHER BENEFITS		———

INDIRECT COSTS OF REMUNERATION

In estimating the indirect costs, in terms of management and employee time spent on remuneration matters, we requested a functional breakdown of the HR department by activity and an estimate of line managers' time spent on, for example, the annual salary review. It was felt by the company project team that at this stage of the project it would be inappropriate to ask line managers how much time they spent on remuneration matters. However, this could be a significant indirect cost to the company and we would therefore recommend analysis be undertaken during Phase 2 of the project.

INDIRECT COSTS

Portion of HR salaries spent on reward matters   ———
Portion of Line Managers' salary spent on reward matters   ———
Employer's Social Insurance (7.65%)   ———

TOTAL INDIRECT COSTS   ———

CONSOLIDATION

The following "cost statement" summarizes the company's compensation and benefits cost for one year, effectively representing its annual investment in the compensation element of its human capital.

DDIRECT COSTS	Cost as % of $ pensionable salary	$
Cash compensation (fixed)		
Cash compensation (variable)		
Social Insurance (average 7.65%)		
Pension benefits		
Other employee benefits		
TOTAL DIRECT COSTS		———
TOTAL INDIRECT COSTS		———
TOTAL COSTS OF REMUNERATION (investment in compensation element of human capital)		———

The figures used (unless otherwise specified) to make our comparisons with "benchmark" data for other companies of similar size (in employee numbers), size, complexity, and sector have been taken from the above table but have excluded indirect costs. A separate benchmark analysis is done on indirect cost against those other companies for which we have performed FCV™ to date.

Pensions

Fit-Cost-Value (FCV™)
Report and Recommendations

The following sample worksheets summarize the key findings and recommendations from a Fit-Cost-Value™ HR self-assessment. A summary is provided for each HR area together with a list of key comments and recommendations, including a suggested time scale for implementation. These sheets are intended to link each stage of the HR strategy review process to the list of conclusions and recommendations to provide a high-level summary of the findings to date.

The FCV™ assessment is intended to determine how well the HR function currently performs in respect of HR policy *costs*, perceived *value* to employees, as well as determining how well the HR service *fits* with the needs of business strategies and best practice in other companies.

KEY TO THE SUMMARY SHEET

- *Cost* and *strategic fit:* **H** = high; **M** = medium; **L** = low.
- *Value:* **A** = wide discrepancy/low desirability (improve or eliminate); **B** = wide discrepancy/high desirability (improve); **C** = narrow discrepancy/low desirability (hold or eliminate); **D** = narrow discrepancy/high desirability (maintain).
- *Operational fit:* This is where the company is assessed against best practice. Characteristics of best practice companies have been detailed according to a scale as follows. Each of the tables gives characteristics that Arthur Andersen believes to be attributed to each level. At "innocence" the company is demonstrating a low alignment to best practice, whereas the company at the "excellence" level is demonstrating a high alignment to best practice. **I** = innocence; **A** = awareness; **U** = understanding; **C** = competence; **E** = excellence.

			HR Area: Pensions
Cost	H		• Pension plan recently redesigned. Actuarial valuation carried out in 1997 disclosed a surplus which is being used to reduce company contributions over time • Relatively high cost due to the high levels of benefits provided
		✔	
	M		
	L		
Value	A		• Pensions have been assessed as "maintain" with fairly high desirability and a low discrepancy between "as is" and "like it to be" • Good appreciation from employees, although cost to company is probably underappreciated
A B	B		
C D	C		
	D	✔	

Fit	Business Strategy	H		• A number of pension plans have been merged into one and as such the overall strategic fit was perceived to be medium • There was a low fit against employees having a stake in the company's success • Several elements of strategic fit were judged to be not applicable
		M	✔	
		L		
	Best Practice Innocence-Excellence Now 0 Future +	I		• The company's existing pension arrangements fall into the best practice fit categories of either Understanding or Competence • The desired future position is to strive for Excellence in all areas of the pension arrangements apart from Value for Money where it was felt that Competence would be sufficient within 2–5 years • Generally adequate operating and administrative procedures/processes but with room for review • Market fit: overall company pensions arrangements are generally in line with market best practice
		A		
		U	0	
		C	0	
		E	+	

Recommendations Approximate Time Frame in Months to Implement	Description	0-6 mo.	6-12 mo.	12-18 mo.
	• Review communication material and expand communications efforts	✔ (1-2)		
	• Review administration arrangements	✔ (3)		
	• Introduce a minimum defined contribution benefit within the existing plan	✔ (3-6)		

Arthur Andersen's Worldwide Human Capital

HCS GLOBAL OFFICE PRIMARY CONTACT LIST
(Alphabetically by Country – or State/Province, Country)

Country (including State/Province)	Local Office	Main HCS Contact	Telephone	Mailing Address
Argentina	Buenos Aires	Silvia N. Corallo	54 (1) 311 6644	C C Central 2897, 1000 Buenos Aires, Argentina
Australia	Adelaide	Christopher C. Sharpley	61 (8) 8217 2800	GPO Box 471, Adelaide, South Australia 5001, Australia
Australia	Brisbane	Richard J. Friend	61 (7) 3309 4488	GPO Box 2461, Brisbane, Queensland 40001, Australia
Australia	Melbourne	Christopher M. Butler	61 (3) 9286 8000	GPO Box 5151 AA, Melbourne, Victoria 3001, Australia
Australia	Perth	Harold S. Payne	61 (8) 9483 2222	PO Box 7125, Cloisters Square, Perth, Western Australia 6850, Australia
Australia	Sydney	Paul A. Ellis	61 (2) 9964 6000	GPO Box 4329, Sydney, New South Wales 2001, Australia
Austria	Vienna	Bernard Vanas	43 (1) 531 33	Auditor Treuhand GmbH, Teinfaltstrasse 8, A-1010 Vienna, Austria
Belgium	Brussels	Oliver M. Faulx	32 (2) 545 30 00	Warandeberg 4 Montagne du Parc, B-1000 Brussels, Belgium
Brazil	Rio de Janeiro	Rubens Branco	55 (21) 559 4241	Praia de Botafogo, 300–7 andar, 22250-040, Rio de Janeiro, RJ, Brazil
Brazil	Sao Paulo	Joao A. Branco	55 (11) 5181 2444	Rua Alexandre Dumas, 1981, 04717-906, Sao Paulo, SP, Brazil
Canada, Alberta	Calgary	W. Gerry Zakus	(403) 298-5916	2100, 355-4 Avenue S.E., Calgary, Alberta, T2P 0J1, Canada

Location	City	Name	Phone	Address
Canada, British Columbia	Vancouver	Robert J. Reid	(604) 643-2522	2000-401 West Georgia Street, Vancouver, BC, V6N 5A1, Canada
Canada, Manitoba	Winnipeg	Jeffrey Koplovich	(204) 944-2331	300 St. Mary Avenue, Suite 500, Winnipeg, Manitoba, R3C 3Z5, Canada
Canada, Ontario	Ottawa	David J. Mason	(613) 787-8200	Constitution Square 12th Floor, 360 Albert Street, Ottawa, Ontario K1R 7X7, Canada
Canada, Ontario	Toronto	Michael A. Spudowski	(416) 941-7801	PO Box 29, Toronto-Dominion Centre, Toronto, Ontario M5K 1B9, Canada
Canada, Quebec	Montreal	David J. Mason	(514) 848-1641	600 de Maisonneuve Blvd. West, 28th Floor, Montreal, Quebec H3A 3J2, Canada
Columbia	Bogota	Luz M. Jaramillo	57 (1) 346 0200	Apartado Aereo 75847, Santafe de Bogotá, DC, Columbia
Croatia	Zagreb	Renata Jencic	385 (1) 4611 456	Vlaska 78, 10000 Zagreb, Croatia
Czech Republic	Prague	Kevin Cornelius	420 (2) 2440 1300	Wirtschaftsprüfungsgesellschaft, (2,4) Arthur Andersen, s.r.o., Husova 5, 110 00 Prague 1, Czech Republic
Denmark	Copenhagen	Marianne Sigfusson	45 (/) 35 25 25 25	PO Box 2662, 2100 Copenhagen 0, Denmark
Ecuador	Quito	Juan Francisco Jaramillo	593 (2) 256-612	PO Box 17-1106465, Quito, Ecuador
Egypt	Cairo	Sherif El Kilany	20 (2) 3362000	PO Box 97, Dokki, Cairo, Egypt
England	Birmingham	Anthony Mehigan	44 (121) 230-2101	One Victoria Square, Birmingham B1 1BD, England
England	Leeds	Bill Holmes	44 (113) 243 8222	St Paul's House, Park Square, Leeds LS1 2PJ, England
England	London	Mike Stanley	00 44 (171) 438 3000	One Surrey Street, London, WC2R 2PS, England
England	Manchester	Don Sutherland	44 (161) 228 2121	Bank House, 9 Charlotte Street, Manchester M1 4EU, England

Country (including State/Province)	Local Office	Main HCS Contact	Telephone	Mailing Address
England	Reading	Michael Stanley	44 (118) 950 8141	Abbots House, Abbey Street, Reading, Berkshire RG1 3BD, England
Finland	Helsinki	Raimo Pallonen	358 (9) 693 631	Kansakoulukuja 1A, 00100 Helsinki, Finland
France	Paris	Edoardo de Martino	33 (/) 1 55 61 10 10	41 rue Ybry, 92576 Neuilly sur Seine Cedex, France
Germany	Berlin	Holly Juday	49 (30) 25471-0	Wirtschafttsprüfungsgesellschaft, Stuerberatungsgesellschaft mbH, Tauentzienstrasse 9, 10789 Berlin, Germany
Germany	Dusseldorf	Christian Dahmen	49 (211) 4958-0	PO Box 320107, 40416 Düsseldorf, Germany
Germany	Frankfurt	David Small	49 (6196) 996-0	PO Box 5323, 65728 Eschborn, Germany
Germany	Hamburg	Hans Heyne	49 (40) 37652-0	PO Box 300120, 20301 Hamburg, Germany
Germany	Munich	Oswald Rohrer	49 (89) 126 97-0	Wirtschaftsprüfungsgesellschaft, Steuerberatungsgesellschaft mbH, Arnulfstraße 126, 80636 Munich, Germany
Germany	Stuttgart	Friedhelm Stock	49 (711) 6149-0	Wirtschaftsprüfungsgesellschaft, Steuerberatungsgesellschaft mbH, Augustenstrasse 7, 70178 Stuttgart, Germany
Greece	Athens	Timos Lizardos	30 (1) 93 02 063	S. Pantzopoulos S. A., Syngrou Avenue 377, 175 64 Athens, Greece
Guatemala	Guatemala City	Taufic J. Aranky	502 (/) 331-6912	Diagonal 6 10-65, Zona 10, Centro Gerencial, Las Margaritas, So. Nivel Torre 1, Guatemala City, Guatemala 01010

Country	City	Contact	Phone	Address
Hong Kong	Hong Kong	Mark J. Blumenthal	852 (/) 2852 0222	GPO Box 3289, Hong Kong, Hong Kong
Hungary	Budapest	Hans-Jurgen Fortsch	36 (1) 451 7100	River Estates, Vácu út 35., 1134 Budapest, Hungary
India	Bangalore	Kunal Kashyap	91 (80) 559 6262	11th Floor, Du Parc Trinity, 17 M.G. Road, Bangalore 560 001 India
India	Bombay	Jairaj Purandare	91 (22) 282 5000	17th Floor, Express Towers, Nairman Point, Bombay 400 021, India
India	Madras	Guatam Benjamin	91 (44) 827-5191	Suite #305, DBS Centre. 31A, Cathedral Garden Road, Madras 600 034, India
India	New Delhi	Mukesh Butani	91 11 375 5000	17th Floor, Jawahar Vyapar Bhawan, STC Building, Tolstoy Marg, New Delhi 110 001, India
Indonesia	Jakarta	Kate T. Walters	62 (21) 575 7999	PO Box 2134, Jakarta 10001, Indonesia
Israel	Tel Aviv	Arie Pundak	972 (3) 511 8222	PO Box 29452, Tel Aviv 61293, Israel
Italy	Rome	Roberto Rocchi	39 (6) 482971	Via Campania 47 00187 Rome, Italy
Italy	Turin	Carlo Bindella	39 (11) 5628007	Studio di Consulena Legale e Tributaria, Via F. Dellala 8, 10121 Turin, Italy
Japan	Tokyo	Eiji Mizutani	81 (3) 5228 1600	Chuo Building, 2-17 Kagurazaka, Shinjuku-ku, Tokyo 162. Japan
Kazakhstan	Almaty	Lisa Gialdini	7 (3272) 60 8520	8-A Melnichnaya Street, 480100 Almaty, Kazakhstan
Korea	Seoul	Hye-Ran Chang	82 (2) 767 9114	Yoido PO Box 537, Seoul, Korea
Latvia	Riga	Uldis Kokins	371 (/) 732 1140	Pulkveza Brieza iela 15, LV-1010 Riga, Latvia
Luxembourg	Luxembourg	Alex Sulkowski	352 (/) 42 22 33-1	PO Box 2381, L-1023 Luxembourg, Luxembourg
Malaysia	Kuala Lumpur	Siew Lin The	60 (3) 255 7000	PO Box, 11040, 50734, Kuala Lumpur, Malaysia

Country (including State/Province)	Local Office	Main HCS Contact	Telephone	Mailing Address
Mexico	Mexico City	Bernd Indlekofer	52 (5) 326 8800	Apartado Postal 10-768, 11002 Mexico, D.F., Mexico
New Zealand	Auckland	John F. Secombe	64 (9) 302 0280	PO Box 199, Auckland 1000, New Zealand
New Zealand	Wellington	Geoffrey D. Nightingale	64 (4) 471 1512	PO Box 10648, Wellington, New Zealand
Norway	Oslo	Ase Bjøntegard	47 (/) 22 92 80 00	PO Box 228-Skøyen, 0212 Oslo, Norway
People's Republic of China	Beijing	Tony K. Kwan	86 (10) 6505 3333	1118 China World Tower, 1 Jian Guo Men Wai Avenue, Beijing 100004, People's Republic of China
People's Republic of China	Shanghai	Nora Wu	86 (21) 6386 6688	19/F Shui On Plaza, 333 Huai Hai Zhong Road, Shanghai 200021, People's Republic of China
Peru	Lima	Andres Valle	51 (1) 221 3260	Casilla Postal, N 1038, Lima, Peru
Philippines	Manila	Orlando Manalang	63 (2) 891 03 07	PO Box 7658, DAPO, Domestic Rd, Pasay City, 1300 Metro Manila, Philippines
Poland	Warsaw	Peter Ferrigno	48 (22) 653 90 00	Al Jana Pawla II 23, 00-854 Warsaw, Poland
Portugal	Lisbon	Adelaide Passos	351 (1) 3816000	Amoreiras, Torre 1-15, 1070 Lisbon, Portugal
Puerto Rico	San Juan	Frank Rivera	1 (787) 759 3025	P.O. Box 362260, San Juan, Puerto Rico 00936-2260
Republic of Ireland	Dublin	William Cunningham	353 (1) 670 1000	Andersen House, International Financial Services Centre, Dublin 1, Republic of Ireland
Republic of Singapore	Singapore	Nurhajati Zainol	65 (/) 220 4377	10 Hoe Chiang Road, #18-00 Keppel Towers, Singapore 0893315, Republic of Singapore
Republic of South Africa	Johannesburg	Carl King	27 (11) 328 3000	PO Box 41294, Craighall 2024, Republic of South Africa

Country	City	Contact	Phone	Address
Romania	Bucharest	Venkatesh Srinivasan	40 (1) 250 9701	International Business Center Modern, BD. Carol I nr. 34-36, etaj 15, Sector 2, Bucharest, 70334, CP 37-36, Romania
Russia	Moscow	Terry Slead	7 (095) 755 9700	Kosmodamianskaya nab. 52/2, 113054 Moscow, Russia
Saudi Arabia	Riyadh	Arfan K. Ayass	966 (1) 478 7801	PO Box 18366, Riyadh 11415, Saudi Arabia
Scotland	Glasgow	Stuart McNab	44 (141) 248 7941	199 St. Vincent Street, Glasgow, G2 5QD, Scotland
Slovakia	Bratislava	David Frier	421 (7) 531 8356	Panska 14, 811 01 Bratislava, Slovakia
Spain	Madrid	Angel Calleja	34 (1) 514 50 00	Raimundo Fernández Villaverde, 65, Edifico Windsor, 28003 Madrid, Spain
Sweden	Stockholm	Bjorn Anderssen	46 (8) 610 58 00	PO Box 23501. S-104 35 Stockholm, Sweden
Switzerland	Geneva	Antonio Maturo	41 (22) 929 42 42	Route de Pré-Bois 29, 1215 Geneva 15, Switzerland
Switzerland	Zurich	Peter Athanas	41 (1) 308 18 88	Binzmühlestrasse 14, 8050 Zürich, Switzerland
Taiwan	Taipei	Eunice Kuo	886 (2) 545 9988	PO Box 1539, Taipei, Taiwan
Thailand	Bangkok	Nickane Suchartaves	66 (2) 280 0900	PO Box, Bangkok, Thailand
The Netherlands	Amsterdam	Jos Beerepoot	31 (20) 503 94 94	PO Box 75381, 1070 AJ Amsterdam, The Netherlands
The Netherlands	Eindhoven	Charles Manuel	31 (40) 245 83 00	PO Box 782, 5600 AT Eindhoven, The Netherlands
The Netherlands	Rotterdam	Martin Meerkerk	31 (10) 242 14 00	PO Box 21937,3001 AX Rotterdam, The Netherlands
Turkey	Istanbul	Nedim Menekse	90 (212) 232 12 10	Danismanlik Ltd Sti., Büyükdere Caddesi Beytem Han. Kat 10 80220, Sisli, Istanbul, Turkey
U.S.A., California	Los Angeles	Peter J. Sutro	(213) 614-6985	633 West Fifth Street, Los Angeles, California 90071
U.S.A., California	San Francisco	James A. Finkelstein	(415) 546-8766	Spear Street Tower, One Market, San Francisco, California 94105

Country (including State/Province)	Local Office	Main HCS Contact	Telephone	Mailing Address
U.S.A., Colorado	Denver	David V. Gutierrez	(303) 291-9436	1225 Seventeenth Street, Suite 3100, Denver, Colorado, 80202
U.S.A., Connecticut	Hartford	Christian L. Lindgren	(860) 280-0783	One Financial Plaza, Hartford, Connecticut 06103
U.S.A., Connecticut	Stamford	John A. Magliano	(212) 708-6406	Champion Plaza, 400 Atlantic Street, Stamford, Connecticut, 06912-0021
U.S.A., District of Columbia	Washington DC	Barry L. Reisig	(703) 734-7354	8000 Towers Crescent Drive, Suite 400, Vienna, Virginia 22181
U.S.A., Florida	Miami	Sandra L. Gaffin	(305) 789-2593	One Biscayne Tower, Suite 2100, Miami, Florida 33133
U.S.A., Georgia	Atlanta	Bruce K. Benesh	(404) 589-4167	225 Peachtree Street, N.E. Atlanta, Georgia 30303
U.S.A., Illinois	Chicago	Marion Gajek	(312) 507-6810	33 West Monroe Street, Chicago, Illinois 60603
U.S.A., Massachusetts	Boston	John K. Dirlam	(617) 330-4540	225 Franklin Street, Boston, Massachusetts 02110
U.S.A., Michigan	Detroit	Scot A. Morrison	(313) 596-7944	500 Woodward Avenue, Suite 2700, Detroit, Michigan, 48226-3424
U.S.A., Minnesota	Minneapolis	Lawrence A. Luebbers	(612) 334-2154	45 South Seventh Street, Minneapolis, Minnesota 55402
U.S.A., Missouri	Kansas City	Timothy K. Plummer	(816) 292-7605	911 Main Street, Suite 1500, Kansas City, Missouri 64105
U.S.A., Missouri	St. Louis	Leslie A. Small	(314) 425-9301	1010 Market Street, St. Louis, Missouri 63101-2089
U.S.A., Nebraska	Omaha	Katherine E. Welch	(402) 449-2240	1700 Farnhma Street, Suite 1800, Omaha, Nebraska 68102
U.S.A., New Jersey	Roseland	James M. Scannella	(973) 403-6407	101 Eisenhower Parkway, Roseland, New Jersey 07068-1099
U.S.A., New Mexico	Albuquerque	Ellen E. Copland	(505) 889-4800	6501 Americas Parkway, NE, Suite 400, Albuquerque, New Mexico 87110

U.S.A., New York	Long Island	Susan M. Mosoff	(516) 385-2683	115 Broad Hollow Road, Melville, New York 11747-4985
U.S.A., New York	New York	James Hatch	(212) 708-6000	1345 Avenue of the Americas, New York, New York 10105
U.S.A., North Carolina	Charlotte	Mark J. Rosen	(704) 332-1384	100 North Tryon Street, Suite 3800, Charlotte, North Carolina 28202-4000
U.S.A., North Carolina	Greensboro	Larry E. Sigmon	(336) 271-3570	301 North Elm, Suite 300, Greensboro, North Carolina 27401
U.S.A., Ohio	Cincinnati	Larry V. Baker	(513) 762-0219	425 Walnut Street, Suite 1500, Cincinnati, Ohio 45202-3912
U.S.A., Ohio	Cleveland	Michael J. Gebura	(216) 348-2709	200 Public Square, Suite 1800, Cleveland, Ohio 44114-2803
U.S.A., Ohio	Columbus	Laura L. Warren	(614) 229-5355	41 South High Street, Suite 2100 Huntington Center, Columbus, Ohio 43215-6150
U.S.A., Ohio	Toledo	Kathryn S. Hoops	(419) 241-8600	300 Madison Avenue, Toledo, Ohio 43604-1586
U.S.A., Oklahoma	Oklahoma City	Patricia K. Biscopink	(405) 231-2231	20 N. Broadway, Suite 600, Oklahoma City, Oklahoma 73102
U.S.A., Oklahoma	Tulsa	George A. Jonas	(918) 746-8121	6450 South Lewis, Suite 300, Tulsa, Oklahoma 74136
U.S.A., Oregon	Portland	Tracy A. Bean	(503) 220-6043	111 S.W. Columbia Street, Suite 1400, Portland, Oregon 97201
U.S.A., Pennsylvania	Philadelphia	Bruce E. Clouser	(215) 241-7376	1601 Market Street, Philadelphia, Pennsylvania 19103
U.S.A., Pennsylvania	Pittsburgh	Larry R. Heckathorn	(412) 232-1294	2100 One PPG Place, Pittsburgh, Pennsylvania 15222
U.S.A., Tennessee	Memphis	Donald B. Carter	(901) 575-9213	100 Peabody Place, Suite 1100, Memphis, Tennessee 38103

Country (including State/Province)	Local Office	Main HCS Contact	Telephone	Mailing Address
U.S.A., Tennessee	Nashville	Charles K. DeBenon	(615) 726-6182	424 Church Street, Suite 1000, Nashville, Tennessee 37219
U.S.A., Texas	Dallas	C. Bob McAndrew	(214) 741-8453	901 Main Street, Suite 5600, Dallas, Texas 75202
U.S.A., Texas	Houston	A. Kent Graham	(713) 237-2706	711 Louisiana, Suite 1300, Houston, Texas 77002
U.S.A., Washington	Seattle	Patrick M. Riley	(206) 233-8303	801 2nd Avenue, Suite 800, Seattle, Washington 98104
U.S.A., Wisconsin	Milwaukee	David J. Bohl	(414) 283-3511	100 East Wisconsin Avenue, Milwaukee, Wisconsin 53202
Ukraine	Kiev	Oleg Klitochenko	380 (44) 462 0555	Ukranian House, 2 Khreshchatyk Street, 252601 Kiev, Ukraine
United Arab Emirates	Dubai	Riad T. Dajani	971 (4) 511-311	PO Box 11615, Dubai, United Arab Emirates
Viet Nam	Ho Chi Minh City	Ruy Y. Moreno	84 (8) 821 00 33	12 Nam Ky Khoi Nghia, Q1, Ho Chi Minh City, Viet Nam

Glossary

In writing this book, we have assumed a certain level of sophistication in the field of human resources, and so have used a considerable amount of jargon. This glossary offers short, informal definitions of some of the more unfamiliar terms we have used. Several of the terms are from our own Human Capital Appraisal™ process—including the basic stages and areas of human capital management. Other terms describe current practices in the human capital domain, as described throughout this book, particularly in Chapter 12. We even offer a definition of the term "human capital" itself! These are all *working* definitions, intended to be useful on the job. Please let us know what we should add or subtract for our next edition!

360 degree feedback. A system for personnel evaluation in which individuals are rated not only by their supervisor(s), but also by their peers and subordinates.

5^2™. A matrix, designed by Arthur Andersen, designed to help in conducting Human Capital Appraisal.™ The 5^2-grid displays the five stages of human capital appraisal along the horizontal line and the five areas of human capital along the vertical line. Intended to show human capital appraisal "at a glance."

Appraisal. The art and science of determining the worth of something or someone.

Arthur Andersen Human Capital Index™. An index now being developed by Arthur Andersen to score companies on the value of their human capital.

Assessment. A stage of appraisal; for example, the second stage of the Human Capital Appraisal™ process.

Benchmarking. Comparing companies with respect to practices, processes, or tasks—or the results accruing from these.

Best practice(s). Actions recommended because of their known success in increasing company value. Best practices are often based on a *benchmarking* process.

Broadbanding. A method of classifying positions in an organization in "broad" or large "bands." Broadbanding has implications for performance management and rewards, and for career development, succession planning, and training.

Capital. Money or other valuable material (including the labor and knowledge base of human resources in a company) that maintains, increases, or decreases in value through management over time.

Career development. A program that helps employees achieve a sense of professional direction by assessing and training employees, and by mapping the opportunities available to them.

Clarification. A stage at the beginning of the Human Capital Appraisal™ process in which managers and other employees determine a company's general strategic direction and assess the degree to which human capital programs are aligned with it.

Coach. The person providing the potential styles and tools for increasing performance. (Industrial Society of the United Kingdom, 1998) Good coaches have direct personal *experience* in the matter being coached and use a number of skills such as listening (being a sounding board), questioning, summarizing, giving actionable feedback, offering encouragement, being an inspiration or model, brainstorming, and joint problem-solving. Line managers are the most likely to be coaches or to identify potential coaches. (See also *Mentor.*)

Coaching. The art of facilitating the learning, performance, and enjoyment of another (The Industrial Society of the U.K. 1998). Coaching aims to improve performance by increasing the self-awareness of the person being coached, and by increasing the person's knowledge and skills in a particular job or task. Coaching can occur as a result of a formal coach/coachee assignment, or it can unfold as an informal event. (See also *Mentoring.*)

Communications. The art and science of conveying information. The term *communications* has two main applications in human capital management. On the one hand, it indicates an ongoing formal company process (often called "employee communications" on an organization chart) that may be improved through clarification, assessment, design, implementation, and monitoring. On the other hand, it signifies the means through which the information and ideas of human capital appraisal may be conveyed (meetings, memos, and the like). So there may be *communications* (meetings and memos) about *communications* (the communications function within a company).

Competency. The set of behavior patterns that the incumbent needs to bring to a position in order to perform its tasks and function at required skill level. (Boam 1992)

Compliance. Conformity to authoritative standards. In human capital appraisal, the formal effort made by a company to comply with all known laws and regulations affecting employment.

Cost. An expenditure of resources; in economics, a measure of human endeavor in monetary units. (Dean 1998)

Design. The creation of products or services (including internal company programs); a necessary stage in the management of any goal-oriented process, including human capital appraisal.

Diversity. Variety of elements; appropriate variety in the age, gender, race, and competencies of the people comprising an organization, including its employees and directors.

Employee relations. A branch of management or management studies that focuses on the relationship between senior management and the other employees. In manufacturing industries, particularly where unions are present, this is called "industrial relations."

Empowerment. A management buzzword used to describe a variety of initiatives aimed at increasing employees' sense of ownership and responsibility for their work.

Enablers. Processes instituted to support a function. For example, the enablers of human capital in a company include mechanisms for legal and accounting compliance, employee relations, communications, and information systems.

FCV™. See *Fit-Cost-Value™.*

Fit. Compatibility or conformity of one thing to another. In the Fit-Cost-Value™ matrix, the dimension that indicates the fit of programs or initiatives with company strategy.

Fit-Cost-Value™ (FCV™) A matrix developed by Arthur Andersen in which human capital programs are plotted to show their level of strategic fit (along one axis) and their level of perceived or known value in relation to cost (along the other axis). See also *Fit, Cost,* and *Value.*

Flexible benefits. Benefits from which an employee may choose.

Flexible work. Alternatives to the traditional nine-to-five, five-day week for an individual. These include job-sharing, part-time or flexible hours, and working from home (telecommuting).

HCE Chart. See *Human Capital Effectiveness™ Chart.*

HRIS. See *Human resources information systems.*

Human capital. Human beings viewed as target for investment in anticipation of returns. In macroeconomics, governments invest in education and training anticipating returns in the form of higher employment rates and other signs of prosperity. In microeconomics, company managements invest in employee programs anticipating returns in the form of higher long-term stock prices and other indicators of company value.

Human Capital Appraisal™. A method created by Arthur Andersen to appraise the value of human capital in an organization.

Human Capital Effectiveness™ Chart (HCE Chart). An Arthur Andersen model showing how a company's Fit-Cost-Value profile compares to peers.

Human resources information system (HRIS). An information system dedicated to conveying information about employment matters. Also called human capital information system (HCIS).

Implementation. Facilitation of a process. In the human capital appraisal process, the stage between design and monitoring.

Induction. See *Orientation.*

Industrial relations. See *Employee relations.*

Job. An individual's paid participation in an organization's process or processes through a relatively stable (although not necessarily fixed) set of tasks and/or competencies.

Job evaluation. Formal evaluation of the tasks performed by an individual and the competencies he or she brings to it.

Learning organization. An organization that emphasizes the importance of learning through programs and other means.

Mentor. An experienced person who guides an inexperienced one, often called a protégé or mentee. (See also *Coach*)

Mentoring. A formal or informal program through which an experienced person guides an inexperienced one. (See also *Coaching*)

Monitoring. Keeping watch over something—especially measuring it against a chosen standard; also, the last stage in the human capital appraisal process.

Multiskilling. Increasing the skills of individuals, especially in order to enable them to exchange tasks and even jobs.

Organizational structure. A map of working relationships in an organization, often visualized as reporting lines.

Orientation. Actions taken to give an individual a sense of direction in a new endeavor. In companies, a program to introduce new employees to their jobs and to the organization.

Outsourcing/Insourcing. The location of those performing work for an organization—either outside as contractors or inside as employees.

Performance management. Programs designed to motivate good performance and discourage poor performance. These programs are often linked to pay.

Process. A related group of tasks that taken together create a result of value to a customer. (Hammer 1996)

Recruitment. The effort to attract candidates for openings in an organization, and the selection of incumbents from this pool of candidates.

Retention. The ability to keep something or someone from leaving. In management, the absence of turnover for a position or positions during a specific period of time.

Retirement. A departure in which the person leaving receives (or would under normal circumstances be qualified to receive) a pension based on years of service.

Rewards. Compensation paid as base salary, bonus pay (pay awarded for past performance, often without prior benchmarks), incentive pay (pay awarded for achievement of a specific benchmark stated in advance), benefits (such as health insurance and pensions), or perquisites ("extras" such as a company car).

Suggestion program. A program through which employees can express their ideas to management, often for a reward.

Task. A unit of work, a business activity normally performed by one person. (Hammer 1996)

Team building. Activities aimed at creating a sense of common purpose in a group.

Teamwork. The accomplishment of tasks through group effort.

Training. Education that prepares an individual for a task, job, or vocation.

Value. The worth of something to someone. In the Fit-Cost-Value™ matrix, the perceived or known value of a human capital program.

Bibliography

Our bibliography has two main parts. Description of Sources acknowledges the sources that were most helpful to us in writing this book. For Further Reading is a series of selected bibliographies listing articles and books on the subject of human capital.

DESCRIPTION OF SOURCES

The original manuscript we wrote had copious notes, reflecting our desire to reference sources. Several readers commented that this made the book look too scholarly—i.e., not practical!—so we eliminated the notes. In lieu of notes, we offer the following Description of Sources organized by chapter. If articles or books do not appear in our bibliographies, we use a long form of citation. If they do appear in the bibliography, we use a short form of citation (last name and year).

Sources for Chapter 1

Readers will note that **Drucker** was careful to use the inclusive term "organizations," rather than the narrower term "company." In our book, we have tried to follow his model, but we often use the word "company" as well because it is simpler, and because the majority of our readers are likely to come from the for-profit sector. The findings and techniques presented in this book apply to the not-for-profit and governmental realms as well. We found this chapter's opening quote in **Reichheld** (1996), p. 92. The source of the "biggest lie" quote was Hammer (1996), p. 118. For the Parable of the Talents, we quote Matthew 25:28-30, *Holy Bible: New Revised Standard Version* (Oxford, U.K.: Oxford University Press, 1989)—but the **King James** version is also worth noting: "Take therefore the talent from him, and give it unto him which hath 10 talents. For unto every one that hath shall be given, and he shall have abundance; but from him that hath not shall be taken away even that which he hath. And cast ye the *unprofitable* servant into outer darkness: there shall be weeping and gnashing of teeth." (Emphasis added.) *The Holy Bible Containing the*

Old and New Testaments Translated out of the Original Tongues and with the Former Translations Diligently Compared and Revised by his Majesty's Special Command, Appointed to be Read in Churches, Authorized King James Version, Printed by Authority (1611). The full quote from **Ptahhotpe** is "Good speech is more hidden than malachite, yet it is found in the possession of women slaves at the millstones." *The Maxims of Ptahhotpe*, ca. 2403 B.C. We traced the etymology of the word capital from **Cotgrave** to **McCullogh** through the *Oxford English Dictionary* (Oxford, U.K.: Oxford University Press, 1971). As an aside, it is interesting to note that Cotgrave's dictionary and the King James translation of the Bible appeared the same year. During this time, the entire lexicon of business was being developed in modern European languages—including the notion of profit, crucial to the concept of human capital. The **Fitz-enz** (1995) quote appears on page 3. Reengineering results are from **Champy** (1995), pp. 2–3. They include decreases in cycle time and costs, and increases in customer satisfaction. The executive quoted was **Clyde W. Moore**, chairman, Crown International, Elkhart, Indiana, who said these words in a small group gathering on October 27, 1997. For more on **Thomson** (1998), see Chapter 12. As Web services add and drop material, the number of Web hits in a search for "human capital" materials fluctuates from day to day, but overall it is growing. On January 1, 1998, America Online's Netscape service listed 1,821,612 sites containing the phrase "human capital." By March 30, 1998 (after rising and falling a few times) the total had grown to 1,947,594. By the time this book is published in late 1998, we expect that the total will stand at over two million. The Website featuring the **Fama-Schwert** (1977) paper is ssb.rochester.edu/fac/Schwert/human.htm. The information on the **Brookings Institution** colloquium came from **James McRitchie**'s Website (corpgov.org) and from an Internet posting by McRitchie (Amazon.com). For more, see **Blair** (1996) in the bibliography of books following. **Frederick Taylor**'s *Principles of Scientific Management* was first published in 1911. For defenses of downsizing as a way to increase the value of human capital, see **Albert J. Dunlap** and **Bob Andelman**, *Mean Business: How I Save Bad Companies and Make Good Companies Great* (New York: Simon & Schuster, 1998), and **Spencer** (1995) in the bibliography of books. Toward the close of this chapter, we mention Nobel Prize–winning economists **Theodore Schultz, Sir Arthur Lewis**, and **Gary Stanley Becker**. See Schultz (1996) and Becker (1995) in the bibliography of books.

Sources for Chapter 2

The news about the Chinese government's downsizing efforts came from **Associated Press** reports retrieved from the Internet in March 1998. A major source for this chapter was **Bryan T. Johnson, Kim R. Holmes** and **Melanie Kirkpatrick**, *1998 Index of Economic Freedom*, Washington, D.C./New York: 1998. Johnson, a policy analyst at the Heritage Foundation, a think tank in Washington, D.C., joined with colleague Holmes and *Wall Street Journal* editor Kirkpatrick to prepare the fourth in a series of annual economic freedom indexes published by the *Wall Street Journal* and the Heritage Foundation. In this chapter, we stated that investment continues in

Southeast Asia. As an example of this, we would cite an early 1998 survey of members of the **Treasury Management Association** in Bethesda, Maryland: Over 90 percent of the respondents reported no change in their companies' further developments in the region. The rest were divided among those who were undecided (2 percent), planning to retrench (3 percent), or planning to expand. The **International Monetary Fund** paper entitled "Aging in the Asian Tigers: Challenges for Fiscal Policy" can be found on the Internet at ideas.uquam.ca/ideas/ data/Papers/fthin-mofu97-143, or more simply, using the search phrase "demographics + aging" on most search engines. Our figure on the high dollar amounts spent in technology consulting came from **Tim Bourgeois,** director of the Kennedy Research Group in Fitzwilliam, Massachusetts, which tracks the consulting industry, cited in the "Management Letter" column in the *Wall Street Journal,* February 5, 1998, p. A-1. For more on workforce shortages, see **Kolberg** and **Smith** (1991) in the bibliography of books (microeconomic), who correctly predicted "an acute shortage of skilled employees." General comments on workforce demographics in the United Kingdom were based in part on Richard Pearson, "The Challenge of Diversity," *Human Resources,* November/December 1996, pp. 135–40. Comments on EU trends for recruitment of older people came from "Riches in Our Midst: Older People in the Workplace," *Human Resource Management,* Spring/Summer 1995, pp. 13–15. A final note: For an interesting example of the increasing return or growth theory of economics applied to human capital, see **Arvid** (1992) in the bibliography of books. Sample chapter titles in Arvid include: Nonlinear Causality: An Introduction to Higher Analysis of Causal Processes, Causality in Bounded Dynamics: Full Predictability Or Chaos, Causality in Unbounded Dynamics: Self-steering, and Economic Causality: The Reduction to Human Capital. Arvid's book will be appreciated by economists and others who are interested in complex adaptive systems. For more on the general subject of the new economics of growth based on increasing returns, contact the **Santa Fe Institute** in Santa Fe, New Mexico, the world's leading center for studies in complexity.

Sources for Chapter 3

The **William James** quote is from *Pragmatism* (1907). Our statement on the limits of human ability to process information is backed by **George A. Miller**'s widely cited article, "The Magic Number Seven, Plus or Minus Two: Some Limits on Our Capacity for Processing Information," *Psychological Review,* Vol. 63, No. 2 (1956), pp. 81–97.

Sources for Chapter 4

Our quote on the strategic role of human relations came from **Christopher Mabey** and **Paul Iles,** "The Strategic Integration of Assessment and Development Practices: Succession Planning and New Manager Development," *Human Resource Management Journal,* Vol. 3, No. 4 (1995), pp. 16–34. For more on this article, see Chapter 8. For a good example of a strategy that includes a reward component, see

"AT&T: New Boss, New Strategy. Will It Work? A Talk with CEO Mike Armstrong," the cover story of the February 2, 1998, *Business Week*, pp. 122 ff. We acknowledge a debt to the **Industrial Society of the United Kingdom** for the 1994 study quoted.

Sources for Chapter 5

In constructing the "red flags" checklist for Chapter 5, we drew primarily from our own experience, but also found certain books and articles particularly informative. In the section Appraising the Programs for Recruitment, Retention, and Retirement, several sources got our attention. In the section on appraising recruitment programs we warn against undue focus on employer references. This was based in part on learning about a Robert Half survey on the limitations of employer references and Nissan's use of psychometric testing. Our source was the "Recruitment" section of *Human Resources Management*, Spring/Summer 1995, pp. 9–10. We confirmed our belief in the importance of bias-free recruitment by reading "The Challenge of Diversity," *Human Resources*, November/December 1996, pp. 135–40. Our warning against age bias was inspired in part from learning about certain trends in this regard, including age bias in the United Kingdom. Our source here was "Riches in Our Midst: Older People in the Workplace" (1995), cited above for Chapter 2. In the training section, we mentioned training in hospitality. This is based on an actual example: a **Hyatt Hotels** training program that teaches basic human courtesies such as smiling! Our source is close to home: **Robert Hiebeler, Thomas B. Kelly,** and **Charles Ketteman,** *Best Practices: Building Your Business with Customer-Focused Solutions* (New York: Simon & Schuster, 1998), p. 183.

Sources for Chapter 6

If the reader has a sense of déjà vu in reading this chapter, it may be because some of the Arthur Andersen partners authoring this book have published in this area. See **Friedman** (1990) and **Walker** (1997) in the bibliography of books. Also of note is an article by **Hatch** and **Nemerov** (1997), listed in the Andersen article bibliography. Our discussion of designing retention programs mentions the importance of designing recruitment programs linked to strategy. For more on this, see **Gubman** (1998) in the bibliography of books. Readers should note that this chapter is based on the actual, documented experience of many real companies. For example, in the flexible benefits area, companies using a stakeholder-based approach in design include **Colgate-Palmolive Ltd., Royal Mail,** and **Scottish and Newcastle Retail.** The Eliot lines are from "The Hollow Men" (1925).

Sources for Chapter 7

Many of the implementation principles discussed in this chapter were based on the experiences of the Best Practice Companies with which we have worked, as detailed in Chapter 12.

Sources for Chapter 8

In the beginning of this chapter, we note that our partners have been involved in setting accounting standards. Exemplary in this regard is **Edmond L. Jenkins,** former managing partner of the Professional Standards Group of Arthur Andersen, who will be serving as the chairman of the **Financial Accounting Standards Board** (FASB) until 2002. The FASB sets accounting standards for public companies in the United States. Its work is augmented by the private sector **Committee of Sponsoring Organizations** (COSO), which began as the **National Commission on Fraudulent Financial Reporting,** chaired by **James C. Treadway,** a lawyer who served as a member of the **U.S. Securities and Exchange Commission.** After the Treadway Commission published its report on fraud in 1987, its work continued under COSO, whose full name is the Committee of Sponsoring Organizations of the Treadway Commission. Sponsors are the **American Institute of Certified Public Accountants,** the **American Accounting Association,** the **Institute of Internal Auditors,** the **Institute of Management Accountants,** and the **Financial Executives Institute. David L. Landsittel,** managing director of auditing at **Arthur Andersen,** Chicago, served on the eight-member Project Advisory Council of COSO for the Internal Control-Integrated Framework project. On the subject of systems, we quoted **Robert Simons** and **Antonio Davila,** "How High is Your Return on Management?" *Harvard Business Review,* January/February 1998, pp. 71–80. The point about systems appears on page 74 of their article.

Sources for Chapter 9

In this chapter once again we quote **Mabey** and **Iles** (1995). The **Arthur Andersen** Global Best Practices database mentioned in the chapter was developed with the **International Benchmarking Clearing House,** a Houston-based nonprofit.

Sources for Chapter 10

The section on labor costs is based in part on an article entitled "Measuring and Evaluating Human Capital," by **Jac Fitz-enz,** which appeared in a book sponsored by Arthur Andersen entitled *The HR Director* (New York: Profile Pursuit, 1997), pp. 25–29. Figures 10-1 and 10-2 are based in part on figures in this article, but with more explicit math and plainer labeling. For more writings by Dr. Fitz-enz, see the bibliography of books. As mentioned, **Edwin Dean**'s materials on cost appear on his Website (http:/akao.larc.nasa.gov).

Sources for Chapter 11

In the beginning of this chapter, we cite **Gary Stanley Becker** (1993). His book on human capital includes the following chapters of interest: Human Capital Revisited, Investment in Human Capital: Effects on Earnings, and Investment in Human Capital: Rates of Return. The AICPA principles we quoted came from **Maurice**

Moonitz, "The Basic Postulates of Accounting," *Accounting Research Study Number 1* (American Institute of Certified Public Accountants, 1961), p. 23.

Sources for Chapter 12

These "best practice" cases are based on information made available (with permission) by the **Industrial Society of the United Kingdom** or other outside sources such as the **Income Data Services** (IDS), a research group that provides pan-European income information.

In alphabetical order by company, the references are as follows:

Avis, Industrial Society (Volume 8, pp. 18–19)

Body Shop International, Industrial Society (Volume 21, pp. 18–19)

BP Chemical, Industrial Society (Volume 8, pp. 20–21)

British Petroleum, Industrial Society (Volume 8, pp. 20–21)

BT plc, IDS study 573/March 1995, page 9

BT plc, Industrial Society (Volume 4, pp. 20–21)

BT plc, Industrial Society (Volume 12, pp. 20–21)

Colgate-Palmolive, Industrial Society (Volume 34, pp. 14–15)

Ericsson Ltd, Industrial Society (Volume 28, pp. 22–23)

Glaxo Wellcome, Industrial Society (Volume 27, pp. 22–23)

IBM, Industrial Society (Volume 1, pp. 20–21)

Kodak, Industrial Society (Volume 36, pp. 18–19)

Land Rover Vehicles, Industrial Society (Volume 4, pp. 24–25)

One2One, Industrial Society (Volume 17, pp. 26–27)

Royal Bank of Scotland, Industrial Society (Volume 30, pp. 30–31)

Royal Mail, Industrial Society (Volume 34, pp. 20–21)

Stamco, Industrial Society (Volume 8, pp. 26–27)

Tesco, Industrial Society (Volume 4, pp. 26–27)

Unilever plc, Industrial Society (Volume 28, pp. 28–29)

Vauxhall Motors, IDS study 573/March 1995 pp. 20–21

This chapter contains no confidential information. Sales figures given are the most recent figures available. Public company sales figures are based on information in *Nelson's Directory of Investment Research* (Port Chester, NY: Nelson Information Inc., 1998), Volumes 1 (U.S.) and II (International), and the *Directory of Corporate Affiliations* (New York: National Register Publishing Company, 1997). Databases consulted included Disclosure, Amadeus, and Dun & Bradstreet. We also consulted the *Directory of Corporate Affiliations*. The Parable of the Sower is from the New Testament of the Bible, Luke 8: 5-8, as translated in the *New American Bible,* 1971.

FOR FURTHER READING

We have listed below articles and books for further reading on the subject of human capital. Articles are from a list identified by Lexis-Nexis as mentioning human capital eight times or more. (A note for the sticklers: With only a few exceptions, this resource provided only starting page numbers. Since we could not obtain all the articles to complete the citations, we have simplified all citations using the "ff." convention for continued pages.)

Books are selected from a list of books recommended by Amazon.com on the subject of human capital, along with a few of our own recommendations.

We have arranged entries into two categories: macroeconomic and microeconomic. Articles in the macroeconomic category will be more interesting to public sector policymakers, while articles in the microeconomic category will be more relevant to private sector managers.

The final section of the bibliography is a list of Arthur Andersen material appearing in the *HR Director* series published by Profile Pursuit, based in London and New York. For this resource, which we have at hand, full page information is provided.

Articles: Macroeconomic

Alba-Ramirez, Alfonso. "Formal Training, Temporary Contracts, Productivity and Wages in Spain." *Oxford Bulletin of Economics & Statistics*, Vol. 56, No. 2 (May 1994), 151ff.

Anderson, Deborah, and Shapiro, David. "Racial Differences in Access to High-paying Jobs and the Wage Gap between Black and White Women." *Industrial and Labor Relations Review*, Vol. 49, No. 2 (January 1996), 273ff.

Arnold, Lutz G. "Growth, Welfare, and Trade in an Integrated Model of Human-Capital Accumulation and Research." *Journal of Macroeconomics*, Vol. 20, No. 1 (Winter 1998), 1ff.

Baimbridge, Mark, and Simpson, Claire. "Rewards to Academia: The Remuneration of Vice Chancellors and Principals." *Applied Economics*, Vol. 28, No. 6 (June 1996), 631ff.

Baldi, Stephane, and McBrier, Debra Branch. "Do the Determinants of Promotion Differ for Blacks and Whites?" *Work & Occupations*, Vol. 24, No. 4 (November 1997), 478ff.

Barron, John M., Black, Dan A., and Loewenstein, Mark A. "Gender Differences in Training, Capital, and Wages." *Journal of Human Resources*, Vol. 28, No. 2 (March 22, 1993), 343ff.

Becker, Elizabeth, and Lindsay, Cotton M. "Male/Female Disparity in Starting Pay." *Southern Economic Journal*, Vol. 61, No. 3 (January 1995), 628ff.

Becker, Gary S. "Human Capital: One Investment Where America Is Way Ahead." *Business Week*, March 11, 1996, 18ff.

Blair, Margaret M. "Corporate 'Ownership.'" *Brookings Review*, Vol. 13, No. 1 (January 1995), 16ff.

Blau, Francine D., and Ferber, Marianne A. "Career Plans and Expectations of Young Women and Men: The Earnings Gap and Labor Force Participation." *Journal of Human Resources*, Vol. 26, No. 1 (September 22, 1991), 581ff.

Bonache, Jaime, and Cervino, Julio. "Global Integration Without Expatriates." *Human Resource Management Journal*, Vol. 7, No. 3 (1997), 89ff.

Borland, Jeff, and Suen, Anthony. "The Experience-Earnings Profile in Australia." *Economic Record*, Vol. 70, No. 208 (March 1994), 44ff.

Bovenberg, Lans, and Van der Linden, Anja. "Pension Policies and the Aging Society; Organization for Economic Cooperation and Development Countries." *OECD Observer*, No. 205 (April 14, 1997), 10ff.

Broadbridge, Adelina. "Why Earnings Differentials Are Different for Men and Women in Retailing." *Service Industries Journal*, Vol. 17, No. 2 (April 1997), 221ff.

Caballe, Jordi. "Endogenous Growth, Human Capital and Bequests in a Life-cycle Model." *Oxford Economic Papers*, Vol. 47, No. 1 (January 1995), 156ff.

Carlino, Gerald A. "Do Education and Training Lead to Faster Growth in Cities?" *Business Review* (Federal Bank of Philadelphia), Vol. 90, No. 2 (January/February 1995), 15ff.

Carnevale, David G. "A Symposium: The Human Capital Challenge in Government." *Review of Public Personnel Administration,* Vol. 16, No. 3 (Summer 1996), 5ff.

Chandrasekhar, Jai K. "Worker Empowerment Through Corporate Law?" *Yale Law Journal,* Vol. 105, No. 6 (April 1996), 1707ff.

Clark, Robert L., and Ogawa, Naohiro. "The Effect of Mandatory Retirement on Earning Profiles in Japan." *Industrial and Labor Relations Review,* Vol. 45, No. 2 (January 1992), 258ff.

Cregan, Christina. "Young Workers and Quit Behavior." *Applied Economics,* Vol. 25, No. I (January 1993), 25ff.

Crossley, Thomas F., Jones, Stephen R. G., and Kuhn, Peter. "Gender Differences in Displacement Cost: Evidence and Implications." *Journal of Human Resources,* Vol. 29, No. 2 (March 22, 1994), 461ff.

Daley, Dennis M. "Paths of Glory and the Glass Ceiling: Differing Patterns of Career Advancement Among Women and Minority Federal Employees." *Public Administration Quarterly,* Vol. 20, No. 2 (Summer 1996), 143ff.

Darity, William Jr., Guilkey, David K., and Winfrey, William. "Explaining the Differences in Economic Performance Among Racial and Ethnic Groups in the USA: The Data Examined." *American Journal of Economics & Sociology,* Vol. 55, No. 4 (October 1996), 411ff.

Dolinsky, Arthur L., Caputo, Richard K., Pasumarty, Kishore, and Quazi, Hesan. "The Effects of Education on Business Ownership: A Longitudinal Study of Women." *Entrepreneurship: Theory and Practice,* Vol. 18, No. 1 (September 22, 1993), 43ff.

Dolton, Peter J., and Kidd, Michael P. "Occupational Access and Wage Discrimination." *Oxford Bulletin of Economics & Statistics,* Vol. 56, No. 4 (November 1994), 457ff.

Duncan, Kevin C. "Gender Differences in the Effect of Education on the Slope of Experience-Earning Profiles: National Longitudinal Survey of Youth." *American Journal of Economics & Sociology,* Vol. 55, No. 4 (October 1996), 457ff.

Ermisch, John F., and Wright, Robert E. "Wage Offers and Full-time and Part-time Employment by British Women." *Journal of Human Resources,* Vol. 28, No. 1 (January 1993), 111ff.

Fallick, Bruce C. "A Review of the Recent Empirical Literature on Displaced Workers." *Industrial and Labor Relations Review,* Vol. 50, No. I (October 1996), 5ff.

Farmer, Amy, and Terrell, Dek. "Discrimination, Bayesian Updating of Employer Beliefs, and Human Capital Accumulation." *Economic Inquiry,* Vol. 34, No. 2 (April 1996), 204ff.

Filer, Randall K. "The Usefulness of Predicted Values for Prior Work Experience in Analyzing Labor Market Outcomes for Women." *Journal of Human Resources,* Vol. 28, No. 3 (June 22, 1993), 519ff.

Folbre, Nancy. "Engendering Economics: New Perspectives on Women, Work, and Demographic Change." *World Bank Research Observer,* Annual Conference Supplement (1995), 127ff.

Foster, Andrew D., and Rosenzweig, Mark R. "Information, Learning, and Wage Rates in Low-Income Rural Areas." *Journal of Human Resources,* Vol. 28, No. 4 (September 22, 1993), 759ff.

Fratoe, Frank A. "Rural Minority Business Development." *Review of Black Political Economy,* Vol. 22, No. 2 (September 22, 1993), 41ff.

Gabriel, Paul E., and Schmitz, Susanne. "Favorable Self-selection and the Internal Migration of Young White Males in the United States." *Journal of Human Resources,* Vol. 30, No. 3 (June 1995), 640ff.

Gang, Ira N., and Stuart, Robert C. "What Difference Does a Country Make? Earnings by Soviets in the Soviet Union and in the United States." *Quarterly Review of Economics and Finance,* Vol. 37 (January 1, 1997), 345ff.

Gattiker, Urs E., and Cohen, Aaron. "Gender-based Wage Differences: The Effects of Occupation and Job Segregation in Israel." *Industrial Relations* (Canada), Vol. 52, No. 3 (June 22, 1997), 507ff.

Green, Francis. "The Determinants of Training of Male and Female Employees in Britain." *Oxford Bulletin of Economics & Statistics*, Vol. 55, No. I (February 1993), 103ff.

Groot, Wim. "The Incidence of, and Returns to Overeducation in the UK." *Applied Economics*, Vol. 28, No. 10 (October 1996), 1345ff.

Gullason, Edward T. "The Effect of Job Tenure on the Earnings of Women." *Atlantic Economic Journal*, Vol. 19, No. 2 (June 1991), 21ff.

Haque, Nadeem U., and Kim, Se-Jik. "'Human Capital Flight': Impact of Migration on Income and Growth." *International Monetary Fund Staff Papers*, Vol. 42, No. 3 (September 1995), 577ff.

Hellerstein, Judith K., and Neumark, David. "Are Earnings Profiles Steeper Than Productivity Profiles? Evidence from Israeli Firm-level Data." *Journal of Human Resources*, Vol. 30, No. 1 (January 1995), 89ff.

Hersch, Joni, and Davis, Patti. "Job Matching and Women's Wage-Tenure Profile." *Applied Economics*, Vol. 26, No. 3 (March 1994), 205ff.

Kidd, Michael P., and Shannon, Michael. "The Gender Wage Gap: A Comparison of Australia and Canada." *Industrial and Labor Relations Review*, Vol. 49, No. 4 (July 1996), 729ff.

Kiker, B.F., and de Oliveira, M. Mendes. "Optimal Allocation of Time and Estimation of Market Wage Functions." *Journal of Human Resources*, Vol. 27, No. 3 (June 22, 1992), 445ff.

Landau, Daniel L. "Government Expenditure, Human Capital Creation, and Economic Growth." *Journal of Public Budgeting, Accounting & Financial Management*, Vol. 9, No. 3, 467ff.

Lawless, Jim. "Human Capital Is Dominant Asset for Young Families." *Des Moines Register*, August 7, 1996, 512ff.

Lucifora, Claudio. "Inter-industry and Occupational Wage Differentials in Italy." *Applied Economics*, Vol. 25, No. 8 (August 1993), 1113ff.

Maglen, L. R. "The Role of Education and Training in the Economy." *Australian Economic Review*, No. 110 (Second Quarter, 1995), 128ff.

Mahony, Mary, and Wagner, Karin. "Relative Productivity Levels: UK and German Manufacturing Industry." *International Journal of Manpower*, Vol. 16, No. 1 (1995), 521ff.

Melamed, Tuvia. "Career Success: An Assessment of a Gender-specific Model." *Journal of Occupational and Organizational Psychology*, Vol. 69, No. 3 (September 1996), 217ff.

Meng, Xin. "An Examination of Wage Determination in China's Rural Industrial Sector." *Applied Economics*, Vol. 28, No. 6 (June 1996), 715ff.

Neuman, Shoshana, and Silber, Jacques G. "Wage Discrimination Across Ethnic Groups: Evidence from Israel." *Economic Inquiry*, Vol. 34, No. 4 (October 1996), 648ff.

OECD Economic Surveys. "Education and Training: Finland." August 1996, p. 84.

Park, Walter G., and Brat, David A. "Cross-country R&D and Growth: Variations on a Theme of Mankiw-Romer-Weil." *Eastern Economic Journal*, Vol. 22, No. 3 (Summer 1996), 345–54ff.

Park, Walter G., and Ginarte, Juan Carlos. "Intellectual Property Rights and Economic Growth." *Contemporary Economic Policy*, Vol. 15, No. 3 (July 1997), 51ff.

Renkow, Mitch. "Income Non-convergence and Rural-Urban Earnings Differentials: Evidence from North Carolina." *Southern Economic Journal*, Vol. 62, No. 4 (April 1996), 1017ff.

Robst, John. "Post-school Investment and Wage Differentials: Some Further Evidence." *Southern Economic Journal*, Vol. 61, No. 1 (July 1994), 121ff.

Rossenzweign, Mark R., and Wolpin, Kenneth I. "Are There Increasing Returns to the Intergenerational Production of Human Capital? Maternal Schooling and Child Intellectual Achievement." *Journal of Human Resources*, Vol. 29, No. 2 (March 22, 1994), 670ff.

Rubio, Mauricio. "Perverse Social Capital—Some Evidence from Colombia." *Journal of Economic Issues*, Vol. 31, No. 3 (September 1997), 805ff.

Schultz, T. Paul. "Investments in the Schooling and Health of Women and Men: Quantities and Returns." *Journal of Human Resources*, Vol. 28, No. 4 (September 22, 1993), 694ff.

Suliman, Osman. "Innovation and Weak Labor Disposability: Some Theoretical and Empirical Evidence." *Applied Economics*, Vol. 29, No. 12 (December 1997), 1687ff.

Waldfogel, Jane. "The Price of Motherhood: Family Status and Women's Pay in a Young British Cohort." *Oxford Economic Papers*, Vol. 47, No. 4 (October 1995), 584ff.

Wang, Ping, and Yip, Chong K. "Macroeconomic Effects of Factor Taxation with Endogenous Human Capital Evolution: Theory and Evidence." *Southern Economic Journal*, Vol. 61, No. 3 (January 1995), 803ff.

Articles: Microeconomic

Anker, Richard. "Theories of Occupational Segregation by Sex: An Overview." *International Labor Review*, Vol. 136, No. 3 (Autumn 1997), 147ff.

Aryee, Samuel, Wyatt, Thomas, and Stone, Raymond. "Early Career Outcomes of Graduate Employees: The Effect of Mentoring and Ingratiation." *Journal of Management Studies*, Vol. 33, No. 1 (January 1996), 95ff.

Association Management. "Managing the Healthy Association: Interview with Robert Rosen." Vol. 45, No. 8 (August 1993), 52ff.

Baldi, Stephane, and McBrier, Debra Branch. "Do the Determinants of Promotion Differ for Blacks and Whites? Evidence from the U.S. Labor Market." *Work & Occupations*, Vol. 4, No. 4, 478ff.

Balfour, Danny L., and Neff, Donna M. "Predicting and Managing Turnover in Human Service Agencies: A Case Study of an Organization in Crisis." *Public Personnel Management*, Vol. 22, No. 3 (September 22, 1993), 473ff.

Bodie, Zvi, and Crane, Dwight B. "Personal Investing, Advice, Theory, and Evidence." *Financial Analysts Journal*, Vol. 53, No. 6 (November–December 1997), 13ff.

Bond, David. "Human Capital Has No Absolute Standard." *Vancouver Sun*, June 5, 1996, D2ff.

Bontis, Nick. "There Is a Price on Your Head: Managing Intellectual Capital Strategically." *Business Quarterly*, Vol. 60, No. 4 (June 22, 1996), 40ff.

Boot, Arnoud W.A. "Why Hang On to Losers? Divestitures and Takeovers." *Journal of Finance*, Vol. 47, No. 4 (September 1992), 1401ff.

Bouillon, Marvin L., Doran, B. Michael, and Orazem, Peter F. "Human Capital Investment Effects on Firm Returns." *Journal of Applied Business Research*, Vol. 12, No. I (Winter 1995/1996), 30ff.

Burt, Tim. "How Holes Help Support Structure." *Financial Times* (London), May 10, 1996, 16ff.

Carrington, William J., and Troske, Kenneth R. "Gender Segregation in Small Firms." *Journal of Human Resources*, Vol. 30, No. 3 (June 1995), 503ff.

Changanti, Rajeswararao, DeCarolis, Dona, and Deeds, David. "Predictors of Capital Structure in Small Ventures." *Entrepreneurship: Theory and Practice*, Vol. 20, No. 2 (December 1995), 7ff.

Chauvin, Keith W., and Ash, Ronald A. "Gender Earnings Differentials in Total Pay, Base Pay, and Contingent Pay." *Industrial and Labor Relations Review*, Vol. 47, No. 4 (July 1994), 634ff.

Cline, Roger S. "The Value of Human Capital: Human Resource Management in the Hotel Industry." *Lodging Hospitality*, Vol. 53, No. 10 (October 1997), 20ff.

Coff, Russell W. "Human Assets and Management Dilemmas: Coping with Hazards on the Road to Resource-Based Theory." *Academy of Management Review*, Vol. 22, No. 2 (April 1997), 374ff.

Couch, Kenneth A. "German Apprenticeship Experience: A Comparison of School-to-Work Models." *Current*, No. 362 (May 1994), 11ff.

Datta, Sudip, Iskander-Datta, Mai E., and Zychowicz, Edward J. "Managerial Self-interest, Pension Financial Slack and Corporate Pension Funding." *Financial Review*, Vol. 31, No. 4 (November 1996), 695ff.

Duleep, Harriet Orcutt, and Regets, Mark C. "Social Security and Immigrant Earnings." *Social Security Bulletin*, Vol. 59, No. 2 (June 1996), 20ff.

The Economist. "Schools Brief—Investing in People." March 26, 1994, 85ff.

Frazis, Harley. "Selection Bias and the Degree Effect." *Journal of Human Resources*, Vol. 28, No. 3 (June 22, 1993), 538ff.

Friedman, Raymond A., and Krackhardt, David. "Social Capital and Career Mobility." *Journal of Applied Behavioral Science*, Vol. 33, No. 3 (September 1997), 316ff.

Fuhrer, Jeffrey C., and Little, Jane Sneddon. "Technology and Growth: An Overview." *New England Economic Review*, November 21, 1996, 3ff.

Garcia-Penalosa, Cecilia. "The Paradox of Education or the Good Side of Inequality." *Oxford Economic Papers*, Vol. 47, No. 2 (April 1995), 265ff.

Garen, John, Berger, Mark, and Scott, Frank. "Pensions, Non-discrimination Policies, and the Employment of Older Workers." *Quarterly Review of Economics and Finance*, Vol. 36, No. 4 (December 1996), 417ff.

Gattiker, Urs E. "Firm and Taxpayer Returns from the Training of Semiskilled Employees." *Academy of Management Journal*, Vol. 38, No. 4 (August 1995), 1152ff.

Gleicher, David, and Stevans, Lonnie K. "Net Employment Reserves and Occupational Wage Rate Determination." *Journal of Post-Keynesian Economics*, Vol. 15, No. 1 (September 22, 1992), 125ff.

Goldberg, Kalman, Highfill, Jannett, and McAssy, Michael. "Technology Choice: The Output and Employment Tradeoff." *American Journal of Economics and Sociology*, Vol. 57, No. 1 (January 1998), 27ff.

Goodwin, Barry K., and Schroeder, Ted C. "Human Capital, Producer Education Programs, and the Adoption of Forward-Pricing Methods." *American Journal of Agricultural Economics*, Vol. 76, No. 4 (November 1994), 936ff.

Greiner, Alfred. "Fiscal Policy in a Model of Endogenous Growth with Learning by Doing." *Public Finance Quarterly*, Vol. 24, No. 3 (July 1996), 371ff.

Groot, Wim, and Mekkelholt, Eddie. "The Rate of Return to Investments in On-the-Job Training." *Applied Economics*, Vol. 27, No. 2 (February 1995), 173ff.

Groot, Wim, Hartog, Joop, and Oosterbeek, Hessel. "Costs and Revenues of Investment in Enterprise-related Schooling." *Oxford Economic Papers*, Vol. 46, No. 4 (October 1994), 658ff.

Haber, Sheldon E., and Goldfarb, Robert S. "Does Salaried Status Affect Human Capital Accumulation?" *Industrial and Labor Relations Review*, Vol. 48, No. 2 (January 1995), 322ff.

Haberfeld, Yitchak, Semyonov, Moshe, and Addi, Audrey. "A Hierarchical Linear Model for Estimating Gender-based Earnings Differentials." *Work & Occupations*. Vol. 25, No. 1 (February 1998), 97ff.

Heckman, James J. "Is Job Training Oversold?" *The Public Interest*, No. 115 (March 22, 1994), 91ff.

Hersch, Joni. "Male-Female Differences in Hourly Wages: The Role of Human Capital." *Industrial and Labor Relations Review,* Vol. 44, No. 4 (July 1991), p. 746.

Hersch, Joni, and Reagan, Patricia B. "Worker Decisions and Efficient Gender-specific Wage-tenure Profiles." *Economic Inquiry,* Vol. 35, No. I (January 1997), 193ff.

Hitt, Lorin M., and Brynjolfsson, Erik. "Information Technology and Internal Firm Organization: An Exploratory Analysis." *Journal of Management Information Systems,* Vol. 14, No. 2 (Fall 1997), 81ff.

Ibarra, Herminia. "Homophily and Differential Returns: Sex Differences in Network Structure and Access in an Advertising Firm." *Administrative Sciences Quarterly,* Vol. 37, No. 3 (September 1992), 422ff.

Ingham, Hilary, and Thompson, Steve. "Mutuality, Performance and Executive Compensation." *Oxford Bulletin of Economics & Statistics,* Vol. 57, No. 3 (August 1995), 295ff.

Investor's Business Daily. "Taxing Human Worth." July 6, 1995, B1ff.

Ippolito, Richard A. "Pensions and Indenture Premia." *Journal of Human Resources,* Vol. 29, No. 3 (June 22, 1994), 795ff.

Jackson, Susan E., and Schuler, Randall S. "Understanding Human Resource Management in the Context of Organizations and Their Environments." *Annual Review of Psychology,* Vol. 46 (January 1, 1995), 237ff.

Jerome-Forget, Monique. "Human Capital: Investing for the Long Term." *Financial Post* (Toronto), June 28, 1997, sec. 1, 22ff.

Johnson, James H., Jr., Bienenstock, Elisa Jayne, and Stoloff, Jennifer A. "An Empirical Test of the Cultural Capital Hypothesis." *Review of Black Political Economy,* Vol. 23, No. 4 (March 22, 1995), 7ff.

Judge, Timothy A., Cable, Daniel M., Boudreau, John W., and Bretz, Robert D., Jr. "An Empirical Investigation of the Predictors of Executive Career Success." *Personnel Psychology,* Vol. 48, No. 3 (Autumn 1995), 485ff.

Jung, Jin Hwa, and Magrabi, Frances M. "Work Experience, Specific Human Capital, and Earnings." *Quarterly Review of Economics and Business,* Vol. 31, No. I (March 22, 1991), 15ff.

Kaestner, Robert, and Solnick, Loren. "Employee Wage Growth Within the Firm: A Deferred Payment of Human Capital." *Applied Economics,* Vol. 24, No. 3 (March 1992), 347ff.

Keith, Kristen, and McWilliams, Abigail. "The Wage Effects of Cumulative Job Mobility." *Industrial and Labor Relations Review,* Vol. 49, No. 1 (October 1995), 121ff.

Kendrick, John W. "Total Capital and Economic Growth." *Atlantic Economic Journal,* Vol. 22, No. 1 (March 1994), 1ff.

King, Mary C. "Human Capital and Black Women's Occupational Mobility." *Industrial Relations,* Vol. 34, No. 2 (April 1995), 282ff.

Kroch, Eugene A., and Sjoblom, Kriss. "Schooling as Human Capital or a Signal: Some Evidence." *Journal of Human Resources,* Vol. 29, No. I (January 1994), 156ff.

Kummel, William. "Pricing, Billing, Compensation, and Ownership: Deconstructing Law Firm Economics." *Accounting for Law Firms,* Vol. 10, No. 12 (December 1997), 1ff.

Laband, David N., and Lentz, Bernard F. "Workplace Mentoring in the Legal Profession." *Southern Economic Journal,* Vol. 61, No. 3 (January 1995), 783ff.

Lado, Augustine A., and Wilson, Mary C. "Human Resource Systems and Sustained Competitive Advantage: A Competency-based Perspective." *Academy of Management Review,* Vol. 19, No. 4 (October 1994), 699ff.

Laing, Derek. "Firm-specific Human Capital as an Employer Discipline Device." *Economic Inquiry,* Vol. 32, No. I (January 1994), 128ff.

Lambert, Richard A., Larcker, David F., and Weigelt, Keith. "The Structure of Organizational Incentives." *Administrative Science Quarterly,* Vol. 38, No. 3 (September 1993), 438ff.

Levine, David. "Can Wage Increases Pay for Themselves?" *Economic Journal,* Vol. 102, No. 414 (September 1992), 1102ff.

Levine, David. "What Do Wages Buy?" *Administrative Science Quarterly,* Vol. 38, No. 3 (September 1993), 438ff.

Liam, Yee. "It's Human Capital That Really Counts." *Business Times* (Malaysia), August 7, 1995, 5ff.

Lindley, James T., Fish, Mary, and Jackson, John. "Gender Differences in Salaries: An Application to Academe." *Southern Economic Journal,* Vol. 59, No. 2 (October 1992), 241ff.

Loh, Eng Seng. "Productivity Differences and the Marriage Wage Premium for White Males." *Journal of Human Resources,* Vol. 31, No. 3 (June 1996), 566ff.

Malos, Stanley B., and Campion, Michael A. "An Options-based Model of Career Mobility in Professional Services Firms." *Academy of Management Review,* Vol. 20, No. 3 (July 1995), 611ff.

Martin, Linda R., and Morgan, Sandra. "Middle Managers in Banking: An Investigation of Gender Differences in Behavior, Demographics, and Productivity." *Quarterly Journal of Business and Economics,* Vol. 34, No. 1 (January 1995), 55ff.

May, Don O. "Do Managerial Motives Influence Firm Risk Reduction Strategies?" *Journal of Finance,* Vol. 50, No. 4 (September 1995), 1291ff.

McMahon, Richard G. P., and Stanger, Anthony M. J. "Understanding the Small Enterprise Financial Objective Function." *Entrepreneurship: Theory and Practice,* Vol. 19, No. 4 (June 22, 1995), 21ff.

McRae, Hamish. "You Can't Put a Value on Human Beings." *Independent* (London), September 24, 1995, 5ff.

Miles, David. "Financial Markets, Ageing and Social Welfare." *Fiscal Studies,* Vol. 18, No. 2 (May 1997), 161ff.

Miles, David. "Pensions Need to Redistribute Human Capital." *Independent* (London), March 17, 1997, 19ff.

Miller, Riel, and Wurzburg, Gregory. "Investing in Human Capital." *OECD Observer,* No. 193 (April 1995), 16ff.

Miller, Shazia Rafiullah, and Rosenbaum, James E. "Hiring in a Hobbesian World: Social Infrastructure and Employers' Use of Information." *Work & Occupations,* Vol. 24, No. 4 (November 1997), 498ff.

Nakosteen, Robert A., and Zimmer, Michael A. "Migration, Age, and Earnings: The Special Case of Employee Transfers." *Applied Economics,* Vol. 24, No. 7 (July 1992), 791ff.

Neumark, David. "Evaluating Age Discrimination Laws: Implications of Age Discrimination in Employment Act." *NBER Reporter,* June 22, 1997, 16ff.

Newman, Meredith Ann. "Career Advancement: Does Gender Make a Difference?" *American Review of Public Administration,* Vol. 23, No. 4 (December 1993), 361ff.

Novos, Ian E., and Waldman, Michael. "Returns to Tenure: Conceptual and Empirical Issues." *Eastern Economic Journal,* Vol. 23, No. 3 (Summer 1997), 337ff.

Odunade, Albert A., and Walsh, Raymond Jr. "Determinants of Female Administrative Support Personnel Compensation at a Large Public University." *Applied Economics,* Vol. 25, No. 9 (September 1993), 1217ff.

Olsen, Reed Neil, and Sexton, Edwin A. "Gender Differences in the Returns to and the Acquisition of On-the-Job Training." *Industrial Relations,* Vol. 35, No. 1 (January 1996), 59ff.

Paci, Pierella, Joshi, Heather, Makepeace, Gerry, and Dolton, Peter. "Is Pay Discrimination Against Young Women a Thing of the Past? A Tale of Two Cohorts." *International Journal of Manpower,* Vol. 16, No. 2 (1995), 60ff.

Pare, Michael. "Invest in State's Human Capital Infrastructure." *Providence Business News,* Vol. 11, No. 28 (October 21, 1996), 2ff.

Paulin, Elizabeth A., and Mellor, Jennifer M. "Gender, Race, and Promotions Within a Private-sector Firm." *Industrial Relations,* Vol. 35, No. 2 (April 1996), 276ff.

Perro, Vincent C. "How Firms Can Increase Their Return on Human Capital." *Investment Dealer's Digest,* March 18, 1991, 18ff.

Posner, Richard A. "What Gets Better with Age? Creativity and Leadership." *Across the Board,* Vol. 34, No. 3 (March 1997), 39ff.

Reilly, Kevin T. "Human Capital and Information: The Employer Size-Wage Effect." *Journal of Human Resources,* Vol. 30, No. 1 (January 1995), 1ff.

Rosen, Howard, executive director, Competitiveness Policy Council. "Prepared Statement before the House Committee on Ways and Means Subcommittee on Trade Investing in Education and Training: Simple Rhetoric or the Key to U.S. Competitiveness? A Survey of U.S. Efforts." *Federal News Service,* July 25, 1996.

Royalty, Anne Beeson. "The Effects of Job Turnover on the Training of Men and Women." *Industrial and Labor Relations Review,* Vol. 49, No. 3 (April 1996), 506ff.

Sandy, Jonathan, and Duncan, Kevin. "Does Private Education Increase Earnings?" *Eastern Economic Journal,* Vol. 22, No. 3 (Summer 1996), 303ff.

Santerre, Rexford E., and Thomas, Janet M. "The Determinants of Hospital CEO Compensation." *Health Care Management Review,* Vol. 18, No. 3 (June 22, 1993), 31ff.

Scarborough, John E. "Measuring Human Life Value from the Courtroom to the Living Room." *Journal of the American Society of CLUs and ChFCs,* Vo. 57, No. 1, 47ff.

Schmitz, Susanne, Williams, Donald R., and Gabriel, Paul E. "An Empirical Examination of Racial and Gender Differences in Wage Distributions." *Quarterly Review of Economics and Finance,* Vol. 34, No. 3 (September 22, 1994), 227ff.

Schuld, Taissia C. A., Schippers, Joop J., and Siegers, Jacques J. "Allocation and Wage Structure: Differences Between Men and Women." *Applied Economics,* Vol. 26, No. 2 (February 1994), 137ff.

Schumann, Paul L., Ahlburg, Dennis A., and Mahoney, Christine Brown. "The Effects of Human Capital and Job Characteristics on Pay." *Journal of Human Resources,* Vol. 29, No. 2 (March 22, 1994), 481ff.

Schwer, R. Keith, and Waddoups, Jeffrey. "On-the-Job Search: The Case of Nevada Test Site Contractor Employees." *Applied Economics,* Vol. 28, No. 11 (November 1996), 1475ff.

Sexton, Edwin A., and Olsen, Reed Neil. "The Returns to On-the-Job Training: Are They the Same for Blacks and Whites?" *Southern Economic Journal,* Vol. 62, No. 2 (October 1994), 328ff.

Shaw, Kathryn. "The Persistence of Female Labor Supply: Empirical Evidence and Implications." *Journal of Human Resources,* Vol. 29, No. 2 (March 22, 1994), 348ff.

Sherer, Peter D. "Leveraging Human Assets in Law Firms: Human Capital Structures and Organizational Capabilities." *Industrial and Labor Relations Review,* Vol. 48, No. 4 (July 1995), 671ff.

Singell, Larry D. Jr. "Managers, Specific Human Capital, and Firm Productivity in Major League Baseball." *Atlantic Economic Journal,* Vol. 21, No. 3 (September 1993), 47ff.

Sloane, P. J., and Theodossiou, L. "Gender and Job Tenure Effects on Earnings." *Oxford Bulletin of Economics & Statistics,* Vol. 55, No. 4 (November 1993), 421ff.

Snell, Scott A., and Dean, James W., Jr. "Integrated Manufacturing and Human Resource Management: A Human Capital Perspective." *Academy of Management Journal,* Vol. 35, No. 3 (August 1992), 467ff.

Solberg, Eric, and Laughlin, Teresa. "The Gender Pay Gap, Fringe Benefits, and Occupational Crowding." *Industrial and Labor Relations Review,* Vol. 48, No. 4 (July 1995), 692ff.

Stevens, Margaret. "A Theoretical Model of On-the-Job Training with Imperfect Competition." *Oxford Economic Papers,* Vol. 46, No. 4 (October 1994), 535ff.

Stewart, Thomas A. "Your Company's Most Valuable Asset: Intellectual Capital." *Fortune*, October 4, 1994, 68ff.

———."A New Way to Think About Employees." *Fortune* (April 13, 1998), 169ff.

Tang, Joyce. "The Model Minority Thesis Revisited." *Journal of Applied Behavioral Science*, Vol. 33, No. 3 (September 1997), 291ff.

Thompson, Alton, and Gray, Benjamin G. "Employment Structure and Poverty: Theoretical Perspectives and Conceptual Frameworks." *American Journal of Agricultural Economics*, Vol. 77, No. 3 (August 1995), 789ff.

Thornburg, Linda. "Accounting for Knowledge." *HR Magazine*, Vol. 39, No. 10 (October 1994), 50ff.

Trostel, Philip A. "The Effect of Deficit Finance on Human Capital." *National Tax Journal*, Vol. 48, No. 4 (December 1995), 531ff.

Truman, Gregory E, and Baroudi, Jack J. "Gender Differences in the Information Systems Managerial Ranks: An Assessment of Potential Discriminatory Practices." *MIS Quarterly*, Vol. 18, No. 2 (June 1994), 129ff.

Variyam, Jayachandran N., and Kraybill, David S. "Small Firms' Choice of Business Strategies." *Southern Economic Journal*, Vol. 60, No. 1 (July 1993), 136ff.

Vella, Francis. "Gender Roles, Occupational Choice and Gender Wage Differential." *Economic Record*, Vol. 69, No. 207 (December 1993), 382ff.

Veum, Jonathan R. "Sources of Training and Their Impact on Wages." *Industrial and Labor Relations Review*, Vol. 48, No. 4 (July 1995), 812ff.

Vohra, Rubina. "How Fast Do We Grow?" *Growth and Change*, Vol. 27, No. 1 (January 1996), 47ff.

Waddoups, Jefrey, Daneshvary, Nasser, and Assane, Djeto. "An Analysis of Occupational Upgrading Differentials Between Black and White Males." *Applied Economics*, Vol. 27, No. 9 (September 1995), 841ff.

Watson, Robert, Storey, David, Wynarczyk, Pooran, Keasey, Kevin, and Short, Helen. "The Relationship Between Job Satisfaction and Managerial Remuneration in Small and Medium-Sized Enterprises: An Empirical Test of 'Comparison Income' and 'Equity Theory' Hypotheses." *Applied Economics*, Vol. 28, No. 5 (May 1996), 567ff.

Weil, Peter A., and Kimball, Peter A. "Gender and Compensation in Health Care Management." *Health Care Management Review*, Vol. 21, No. 3 (June 1996), 19ff.

West, Jonathan P., and Berman, Evan M. "A National Survey: Managerial Responses to an Aging Municipal Workforce." *Review of Public Personnel Administration*, Vol. 16, No. 3 (Summer 1996), 38ff.

Whitely, William T., and Coetsier, Pol. "The Relationship of Career Mentoring to Early Career Outcomes." *Organization Studies*, Vol. 14, No. 3 (June 22, 1993), 419ff.

Winkler, Anne E. "Investment in Women's Human Capital." *Industrial and Labor Relations Review*, Vol. 51, No. 1, 147ff.

Wright, Patrick M., Smart, Dennis L, and McMahan, Gary C. "Matches Between Human Resources and Strategy Among Six Basketball Teams." *Academy of Management Journal*, Vol. 38, No. 4 (August 1995), 1052ff.

Yap, Michael. "The Long and Short of Economic Management." *Business Times* (Malaysia), March 17, 1997, 4ff.

Youndt, Mark A., Snell, Scott A., Dean, James W., Jr., and Lepak, David P. "Human Resource Management, Manufacturing Strategy, Organizational Performance; Special Research Forum: Human Resource Management and Organizational Performance." *Academy of Management Journal*, Vol. 39, No. 4 (August 1996), 836ff.

Zeng, Jinli. "Physical and Human Capital Accumulation, R&D and Economic Growth." *Southern Economic Journal*, Vol. 63, No. 4 (April 1997), 1023ff.

Books: Macroeconomic

Adjibolosee, Senyo B-S. K., editor. *Human Factor Engineering and the Political Economy of African Development.* New York: Praeger, 1996.

Asplund, Rita, editor. *Human Capital Creation in an Economic Perspective.* Berlin /New York: Springer-Verlag, 1996.

Aulin, Arvid. *Foundations of Economic Development.* Berlin /New York: Springer-Verlag, 1992.

Becker, Gary Stanley. *Human Capital: A Theoretical and Empirical Analysis, With Special Reference to Education.* Chicago: University of Chicago Press, 1993.

Becker, Gary Stanley et al. *The Essence of Becker.* Hoover Institution Press Publication No. 426. Stanford, CA: Hoover Institution Press, 1995.

Becker, Gary Stanley. *Accounting for Tastes.* Cambridge, MA: Harvard University Press, 1996.

Begin, James P. *Dynamic Human Resource Systems: Cross-National Comparisons.* De Gruyter Studies in Organization No. 79. Berlin: Walter De Gruyter, 1997.

Behrman, Jere R. *Human Resources in Latin America and the Caribbean.* Washington, D.C.: Inter-American Development Bank, 1996.

Blair, Margaret M. *Wealth Creation and Wealth Sharing: A Colloquium on Corporate Governance and Investments in Human Capital.* Washington, D.C.: Brookings Institution, 1996.

Blaug, Amrk. *The Economic Value of Education: Studies in the Economics of Education.* International Library of Critical Writings in Economics, No. 17. Cheltenham, U.K./Northampton, MA: Edward Elgar Publishing, 1992.

Boam, Rosemary. *Designing and Achieving Competency: A Competency-based Approach to Developing People and Organizations.* New York: McGraw-Hill, 1992.

Brooking, Annie. *Intellectual Capital.* New York: Van Nostrand Reinhold, 1996.

Choukroun, Jean-Marc, and Roberta M. Snow, editors. *Planning for Human Systems: Essays in Honor of Russell L. Ackoff.* Philadelphia: University of Pennsylvania Press, 1992.

Deininger, Klaus W. *Technical Change, Human Capital, and Spillovers in United States Agriculture, 1949–1985.* New York: Garland Publishing, 1995.

Du Roy, Olivier. *The Factory of the Future: Socio-Technical Investment Management European Methods.* Information Booklet Series, Booklet No. 17. Brussels: European Communities, 1992.

Johnes, Geraint. *The Economics of Education.* New York: St. Martins Press, 1993

Johnson, Brian T., Kim R. Homes, and Melanie Kirkpatrick. *1998 Index of Economic Freedom.* Washington, D.C.: Heritage Foundation, 1998.

Judy, Richard W., and Carol D'Amico. *Workforce 2020: Work and Workers in the 21st Century.* Indianapolis: Hudson Institute, 1997.

Locke, Richard, Thomas A. Kochan, and Michael J. Piore, editors. *Employment Relations in a Changing World Economy.* Cambridge, MA: MIT Press, 1995.

Londono, Juan Luis. *Poverty, Inequality, and Human Capital Development in Latin America, 1950–2025.* World Bank Latin American and Caribbean Studies. Washington, D.C.: World Bank, 1996.

Looney, Robert E. *Manpower Policies and Development in the Persian Gulf Region.* New York: Praeger Publishers, 1994.

Mincer, Jacob. *Studies in Human Capital.* Cheltenham, U.K./Northampton, MA: Edward Elgar Pub, 1993.

Mirvis, Philip. *Building the Competitive Workforce; Investing in Human Capital for Corporate Success.* New York: John Wiley & Sons, 1993.

Ogawa, Naohiro et al. *Human Resources in Development Along the Asia-Pacific Rim.* South-East Asian Social Science Monographs. Oxford, U.K.: Oxford University Press, 1993.

Organization for Economic Cooperation and Development (OECD). *Employment and Growth in the Knowledge-based Economy.* Paris: OEDC, 1996.

Schultz, Theodore W. *Origins of Increasing Returns.* Oxford, U.K.: Blackwell Publishing, 1993.

Schultz, T. Paul, Editor. *Investment in Women's Human Capital.* Chicago: University of Chicago Press, 1995.

Swanson, Richard A., and Elwood F. Holton III, editors. *Human Resource Development Research Handbook: Linking Research and Practice.* Berrett-Koehler Organizational Performance Series. San Francisco: Berrett-Koehler, 1997.

Thurley, Keith E. et al, editors. *Work and Society: Labour and Human Resources in East Asia.* Hong Kong: Hong Kong Univ Press, 1996.

Books: Microeconomic

Champy, James. *Reengineering Management: The Mandate for New Leadership.* New York: HarperBusiness, 1996.

Dale, Barrie et al. *Managing Quality and Human Resources: A Guide to Continuous Improvement.* Oxford, U.K.: Blackwell Publishing, 1997.

Dauphinais, William, and Colin Price. *Straight from the CEO.* London: Nicholas Brearley, 1998.

Edvinsson, Leif, and Michael S. Malone. *Intellectual Capital: Realizing Your Company's True Value by Finding Its Hidden Roots.* New York: HarperBusiness, 1997.

Fernandez, John P., and Mary Barr. *The Diversity Advantage: How American Business Can Out-Perform Japanese and European Companies in the Global Marketplace.* New York: Lexington Books, 1993.

Fitz-enz, Jac. *The 8 Practices of Exceptional Companies: How Great Organizations Make the Most of Their Human Assets.* New York: Amacom, 1997.

————. *How to Measure Human Resources Management.* New York: McGraw-Hill, 1995.

Fitzgerald, Robert, and Christopher Rowley, editors. *Human Resources and the Firm in International Perspective.* Cheltenham, U.K. /Northampton, MA: Edward Elgar Publishing, 1997.

Friedman, Brian S. *The Stoy Hayward Guide to Effective Staff Incentives.* London: Kogan Page, 1990.

Griffin, Keith B., and Terry McKinley. *Implementing a Human Development Strategy.* Vol. 1. New York: St. Martins Press, 1995.

Gubman, Edward L. *The Talent Solution: Aligning Strategy & People to Achieve Extraordinary Results.* New York: McGraw-Hill, 1998.

Hambrick, Donald, David A. Nadler, and Michael L. Tushman. *Navigating Change: How CEOs, Top Teams, and Boards Steer Transformation.* Boston, MA: Harvard Business School Press, 1998.

Hammer, Michael. *Beyond Reeingineering: How the Process-Centered Organization is Changing Our Work and Our Lives.* New York: HarperBusiness, 1996.

Hart, Robert A., and Thomas Moutos. *Human Capital, Employment and Bargaining.* Cambridge, U.K.: Cambridge University Press, 1995.

Herriot, Peter et al. *Trust and Transition: Managing the Employment Relationship.* New York: John Wiley & Sons, 1998.

Klein, David A., editor. *The Strategic Management of Intellectual Capital.* Oxford, U.K.: Butterworth-Heineman, 1997.

Kolberg, William H., and Foster C. Smith. *Rebuilding America's Workforce: Business Strategies to Close the Competitive Gap.* Burr Ridge, IL: Irwin Professional Publishing, 1991.

Lazear, Edward P. *Personnel Economics for Managers.* New York: John Wiley & Sons, 1997.

McClelland, Samuel B. *Organizational Needs Assessments: Design, Facilitating, and Analysis.* New York: Quorum Books, 1995.

Miller, Riel. *Measuring What People Know: Human Capital Accounting for the Knowledge Economy.* Paris: Organization for Economic Cooperation and Development, 1996.

Mirvis, Philip H., editor. *Building the Competitive Workforce.* New York: John Wiley, 1993.

Monks, Robert A. G. *The Emperor's Nightingale: Restoring Integrity to the Corporation.* Oxford, U.K.: Capstone, 1998 /New York: Addison-Wesley, 1998.

Monti-Belkaoui, Janice, and Ahmed Riahi-Belkaoui. *Human Resource Valuation: A Guide to Strategies and Techniques.* Westport, CT /New York: Greenwood Publishing Group, 1995.

Nordhaug, Odd. *Human Capital in Organizations: Competence, Training, and Learning.* Oslo, Norway: Scandinavian University Press, 1994.

Pfeffer, Jeffrey. *The Human Equation: Building Profits by Putting People First.* Boston Harvard Business School Press, 1998.

Reichheld, Frederick F. *The Loyalty Effect: The Hidden Force Behind Growth, Profits, and Lasting Value.* Boston: Harvard Business School Press, 1996.

Rosenbluth, Hal F., and Diana McFerrin Peters. *Good Company: Caring as Fiercely as You Compete.* Reading, MA: Addison Wesley, 1998.

Sibson, Robert E. *Strategic Planning for Human Resource Management.* New York: Amacom, 1992.

Sims, Ronald R., and Robert P. Dennehy, editors. *Diversity and Differences in Organizations: An Agenda for Answers and Questions.* New York: Greenwood Publishing Group, 1993.

Spencer, Lyle M., Jr. *Reengineering Human Resources: Achieving Radical Increases in Service Quality—With 50% to 90% Cost and Head Count Reductions.* New York: John Wiley & Sons, 1995.

Stewart, Thomas A. *Intellectual Capital: The New Wealth of Organizations.* New York: Doubleday, 1997.

Thomson, Kevin. *Emotional Capital.* Oxford: Capstone, 1998.

Ulrich, David. *Human Resource Champions: The Next Agenda for Adding Value and Delivering Results.* Boston: Harvard Business School Press, 1997.

Ulrich, David et al., editors. *Tomorrow's HR Management: 48 Thought Leaders Call for Change.* New York: John Wiley & Sons, 1997.

Walker, David. *Retirement Security: Understanding and Planning Your Financial Future.* New York: John Wiley & Sons, 1997.

Selected Arthur Andersen Articles on Human Capital

The following articles all appeared in a series called *HR Director,* published under a special arrangement with Profile Pursuit, Inc., in New York annually and in London semiannually. Since the publisher and the name of the publication are the same in all instances, we will only provide the city, year, and page numbers.

Anderssen, Bjorn. "Norse Code" (re: HR challenges in Scandinavia). London, Autumn /Winter, 1997, pp. 128–33.

Bartlett, Virginia, and Theresa M. Vogler. "Fiduciary Risk Management Today." New York, 1997, pp. 254–55.

Baxter, Gerry. "Sauce for the Goose" (re: outsourcing of HR function). London: Autumn /Winter, 1997, pp. 216–20.

Blackard, Scott. "Traditional and Emerging Health Care Cost Management Strategies." New York, 1997, pp. 283–92.

Brown, Jeff. "Corporate Intranets: Enabling Crucial HR Management Programs in Today's Environment." New York, 1997, pp. 134–44.

Buckalew, Gregg, and Drew Carrington. "Corporate Benefit Plan Decision-Makers Must Define Unacceptable Investment Outcomes (Risk)." New York, 1997, pp. 248–53.

Bumpass, Susan, Constance Filling, and Marshall Gerber. "Trends in Executive Development." New York, 1997, pp. 37–49.

Cohen, Bill. "Claiming a Stake" (re: global share plans). London, Spring /Summer, 1997, pp. 102–108.

—— and Sara Gibbins. "Star Attraction" (re: senior-level pay). London, Spring /Summer 1997, pp. 80–86.

Cook, Paul. "The Move to Defined Contribution Pensions," London, 1996, pp. 24–31.

Cuthill, Sarah. "Total Mobility Management: A Best Practice Approach to International Assignment Policy Development." November, 1997, pp. 261–73.

Fenzel, Patti. "Strategic HR Systems: Critical Issues to Address Before Buying, Building, or Outsourcing Your HRIS." New York, 1997, pp. 99–117.

Friedman, Brian. "Human Capital," London, 1996, pp. 6–11.

—— and Kate Olley. "Human Capital Services," London, Spring /Summer, 1997, pp. 10–12.

—— and Oliver Overstall. "Executive Remuneration." London, 1996, pp. 72–75.

Hamilton-Smith, Karen. "Getting to the Core" (re: outsourcing). London, 1996, pp. 38–45.

——. "Small World." London, Autumn /Winter 1997, pp. 26–32.

Hatch, James. "Integrating People, Process, and Technology." New York, 1997, pp. 60–69.

Hatch, James, and Donald S. Nemerov. "Designing, Communicating, and Implementing a Corporate Compensation Scheme." New York, 1997, pp. 196–200.

Heckathorn, Larry. "Strategic Benefits Outsourcing: A Five-Phase Process." New York, 1997, pp. 81–97.

Hill, Robert. "Culture Clash." London, Spring /Summer, 1997, pp. 94–98.

King, Carl. "Driving Test" (re: company cars). London, Autumn /Winter, 1997, pp. 90–96.

——. "Deals on Wheels." London, Spring /Summer, 1997, pp. 208–12.

Landry, James A. "The Changing Workforce: Implications for Managing Human Capital. New York, 1997, 30–34.

Luebke, Jerry F. "Evaluating the Business Impact of Training Efforts." New York, 1997, pp. 50–59.

McAndrew, Robert. "From Paternalistic to Employee Choice Benefits: Three Requirements for Flexible Benefits in the 21st Century." New York, 1997, pp. 203–15.

McCorkle, Andrew R., and Steven A. Seelig. "Pensions: A New Era of Self-Correction." New York, 1997, pp. 243–47.

Meyer, Bruce M. "Knowledge Management at Arthur Andersen: Technology Creates New Levels of Excellence." New York, 1997, pp. 119–33.

Nadel, Alan A. "How to 'Ease the Squeeze' on Retirement Benefits." New York, 1997, pp. 230–33.

Olley, Kate, and Robert Hill. "Human Assets." London, Spring /Summer 1997, pp. 16–21.

O'Neil, Sandra, and Donald S. Nemerov. "New Wave Compensation." New York, 1997, pp. 184–95.

Overstall, Oliver. "The Balancing Act" (re: scorecard approach to pay). London, 1996, pp. 58–63.

——. "Benchmarking Expatriate Policy." London, Spring /Summer, 1997, pp. 64–69.

Raftery, Tom. "Performance Art" (re: appraisal schemes). London, Autumn /Winter, 1997, pp. 154–60.

Rose, Michael. "Percentage Points" (re: performance-related pay). London, Autumn /Winter 1997, pp. 106–12.

Rosowski, Bob and Jill Carson. "How to Save Times and Money in Acquisitions." New York, 1997, pp. 71–78.

Scott, Caroline. "Going, Going, Gone" (re: impact of new U.K. budget on pensions). London, Autumn /Winter, 1997, pp. 182–87.

Sullivan, James, and Drake Mosier. "The New Retirement Challenge: Educating Employees for Long-Term Security." New York, 1997, pp. 235–41.

Symonds, Ann. "Access Routes" (re: immigration to the United Kingdom). London, Autumn /Winter, 1997, pp. 210–14.

———. "On the Move" (re: immigration to the United Kingdom). London, 1996, pp. 112–17.

Valles, Ellen, and Mike Kesner. "Changing CEO Salary Strategies." New York, 1997, pp. 179–82.

Walker, David M. "The Evolving HR Function and the Need for Human Capital Appraisal." New York, pp. 17–23.

———. "People Management in the 21st Century." New York, 1997, pp. 13–14.

———. "The Looming Retirement Crisis: Implications for Employers, Individuals, and the Nation." New York, 1997, pp. 217–29.

Walsh, Brett. "Human Capital Services" (re: Stage 1 of Human Capital Appraisal). London, Autumn /Winter, 1997, pp. 10–12.

Williams, Mark. "Catch-all: Is Your HR System Truly International?" London, Autumn /Winter, 1997, pp. 40–46.

Woodley, Carol. "End Game" (re: the pension impact of the United Kingdom's 1997 budget). London, Autumn /Winder, 1997, pp. 54–62.

———. "Flexible Benefits." London, 1996, pp. 64–69.

——— and Alan Higham. "A Movable Feast" (re: global pension plans). London, Spring /Summer 1997, pp. 54–59.

Index

About the Authors

Brian Friedman is the worldwide head of Arthur Andersen's Human Capital Services (HCS) practice and is also president of the United Kingdom's Society of Share Plan Practitioners. Mr. Friedman is a leading global authority on a wide range of issues, in particular senior executive compensation and global stock ownership plans. Mr. Friedman is currently working with a number of multinational companies to design innovative and tax-efficient equity structures. Mr. Friedman is a chartered accountant, a member of the Institute of Personnel and Development, and a fellow of the Chartered Institute of Taxation. He is the author of *Effective Staff Incentives*, published by Kogan Page, and *Pay and Benefits Handbook*, published by Tolley.

James Hatch is a partner with Arthur Andersen's Metro New York HCS practice. He has two decades of experience in design and implementation of human resources strategy solutions including: sales force effectiveness, executive compensation programs, change management, total pay design, employee communication, outsourcing, and reengineering. He serves as HCS's global director for people strategy and HR management and as the firm's Northeast HCS consulting practice leader. Mr. Hatch is a certified public accountant with special training in the banking field. Jim has been a lecturer at industry and professional seminars and has published articles on various topics related to human resources strategy, change management, and sales force effectiveness. He is a member of the American Compensation Association and the American Institute of Certified Public Accountants.

David M. Walker is a partner and Managing Director of Arthur Andersen's HCS practice in the U.S./Americas. He also serves as HCS's Global Director for Retirement, Actuarial and Benefits consulting and is a member of the Board of Arthur Andersen Financial Advisors, a registered investment advisor. Before joining Arthur Andersen LLP, Mr. Walker served as U.S. assistant secretary of labor for pension and welfare benefit programs at the U.S. Department of Labor and as acting executive director of the U.S. Pension Benefit Guaranty Corporation. His most recent government position was serving as one of two public trustees for the U.S. Social Security and Medicare Trust Funds from 1990 until 1995. Mr. Walker, who has been a member of a variety of professional, industry, and government commissions and task forces, is a frequent speaker, author, and congressional witness, and is widely quoted in a number of publications on a variety of human capital issues.

A certified public accountant and a registered investment adviser, Mr. Walker is also the author of *Retirement Security: Understanding and Planning Your Financial Future,* published by John Wiley & Sons in 1996.

Printed in the United States
By Bookmasters